ELDER ABUSE AND NEGLECT IN CANADA

by

P. Lynn McDonald
Faculty of Social Work
The University of Calgary

Joseph P. Hornick, Ph.D.
Executive Director of the
Canadian Research Institute
for Law and the Family

Gerald B. Robertson
Professor of Law
The University of Alberta

Jean E. Wallace
Former Senior Research Assistant
at the Canadian Research Institute
for Law and the Family

Butterworths
Toronto   Vancouver

Elder Abuse and Neglect in Canada
© Butterworths Canada Ltd. 1991

Printed and bound in Canada

The Butterworth Group of Companies

Canada	Butterworths Canada Ltd., Toronto and Vancouver, 75 Clegg Road, MARKHAM, Ontario, L6G 1A1 and 409 Granville St., Ste. 1455, VANCOUVER, B.C., V6C 1T2
Australia	Butterworths Pty Ltd., SYDNEY, MELBOURNE, BRISBANE, ADELAIDE, PERTH, CANBERRA and HOBART
Ireland	Butterworths (Ireland) Ltd., DUBLIN
New Zealand	Butterworths of New Zealand Ltd., WELLINGTON and AUCKLAND
Puerto Rico	Equity de Puerto Rico, Inc., HATO REY
Singapore	Malayan Law Journal Pte. Ltd., SINGAPORE
United Kingdom	Butterworth & Co. (Publishers) Ltd., LONDON and EDINBURGH
United States	Butterworth Legal Publishers, AUSTIN, Texas; BOSTON, Massachusetts; CLEARWATER, Florida (D & S Publishers); ORFORD, New Hampshire (Equity Publishing); ST. PAUL, Minnesota; and SEATTLE, Washington

Canadian Cataloguing in Publication Data

Main entry under title:

Elder abuse and neglect in Canada

(Perspectives on individual and population aging series)
Includes bibliographical references and index.
ISBN 0-409-89640-3

1. Aged – Canada – abuse of. 2. Aged – Abuse of.
3. Abused aged – Canada. I. McDonald, P. Lynn.
II. Series.

HV6626.3.E53 1991   362.6   C91-093382-0

Sponsoring Editor — Gloria Vitale
Editor — Julia Keeler
Cover Design — Patrick Ng
Production — Kevin Skinner
Typesetting — Jay Tee Graphics Ltd.

To
Our Families

BUTTERWORTHS PERSPECTIVES ON INDIVIDUAL AND POPULATION AGING SERIES

This Series represents an exciting and significant development for the field of gerontology in Canada. The production of the Canadian-based knowledge about individual and population aging is expanding rapidly, and students, scholars and practitioners are seeking comprehensive yet succinct summaries of the literature on specific topics. Recognizing the common need of this diverse community of gerontologists, Janet Turner, while she was Sponsoring Editor at Butterworths, conceived the idea of a series of specialized monographs that could be used in gerontology courses to complement existing texts and, at the same time, to serve as a valuable reference for those initiating research, developing policies, or providing services to elderly Canadians.

Each monograph includes a state-of-the-art review and analysis of the Canadian-based scientific and professional knowledge on the topic. Where appropriate for comparative purposes, information from other countries is introduced. In addition, some important policy and program implications of the current knowledge base are discussed, and unanswered policy and research questions are raised to stimulate further work in the area. The monographs are written for a wide audience: undergraduate students in a variety of gerontology courses; graduate students and research personnel who need a summary and analysis of the Canadian literature prior to initiating research projects; practitioners who are involved in the daily planning and delivery of services to aging adults; and policy-makers who require current and reliable information in order to design, implement and evaluate policies and legislation for an aging population.

The decision to publish a monograph on a specific topic is based in part on the relevance of the topic for the academic and professional community, as well as on the amount of information available at the time an author is signed to a contract. Because gerontology in Canada is attracting large numbers of highly qualified graduate students as well as increasingly active research personnel in academic, public and private settings, new areas of concentrated research are evolving. Future monographs will reflect this evolution of knowledge pertaining to individual or population aging in Canada.

Before introducing the twelfth monograph in the Series, I would like, on

behalf of the Series' authors and the gerontology community, to acknow-
ledge the following members of the Butterworths "team" and their respec-
tive staff for their unique and sincere contribution to gerontology in
Canada: Andrew Martin, President, for his continuing support of the
Series; Craig Laudrum, Academic Acquisitions Manager, for his enthusias-
tic commitment to the promotion and expansion of the Series; and Linda
Kee, Assistant Vice-President, Editorial, for her co-ordination of the editorial services. For each of you, we hope the knowledge provided in the
Series will have personal value — but not until well into the next century!

Barry McPherson
Series Editor

FOREWORD

Gerontologists, social workers, journalists, lawyers, and health care workers have increasingly expressed concern about the "silent" problem of elder abuse and neglect. Similarly, some members of the research community within the field of gerontology have predicted that the problem will increase as the number of older adults increases. Yet, as we enter the 1990s we still do not know with certainty what constitutes elder abuse or neglect, nor do we have accurate estimates of its incidence or prevalence. Consequently, the public receives inadequate information, which can lead to the perpetuation of myths and stereotypes. This inaccurate information is most likely to be disseminated when the media present an extreme case of abuse or neglect that leads to hospitalization or death. While this "sensational" type of news can raise the sensitivity and consciousness of those concerned with the status and care of older adults, it can also lead to hastily conceived and ill-informed policies and programs for screening, assessment, or intervention. Thus, as we enter the 1990s, and with the hosting of the first national conference on elder abuse and neglect (January 1991), it is essential that the current knowledge base be critically analysed if effective and appropriate policies, programs, and intervention practices are to be initiated in the future.

This monograph, written for professionals, students, researchers, and policy makers in the gerontology, health, legal, and social welfare domains, reviews the growing but diffuse body of literature that has emerged in the past ten years. Much of this literature has considered the problem of abuse as one outcome of stress on caregivers. Hence, the problem is often viewed more from the perspective of the caregiver than from that of the abused older adult. In this monograph, employing a legal and a critical social perspective, the authors stress the need to protect the legal and human rights of the older adult in a potentially abusive situation, or where self-neglect occurs. Thus, the authors constantly raise the possible harmful implications for elderly adults if inappropriate policies, programs, and practices are based on invalid or incomplete theory and research.

The authors, trained in sociology, law, and social work, challenge the reader in Chapter 1 to critically examine the meaning of the various forms and types of abuse or neglect. A taxonomy of elder abuse is introduced, and then both the legal and social definitions of abuse and neglect are described and critiqued. This chapter reviews the characteristics of victims and abusers, and summarizes the reported rates for the incidence and prevalence of abuse. Here, the authors stress the critical difference between studies that employ the absolute number of abused elderly and those that employ the rates of abuse, and indicate the need to distinguish between the incidence (a new occurrence within a specific time frame) and the prevalence (lifetime occurrence) of elder abuse. This chapter also sensitizes the reader to the problems of reliability and validity that can be created by evidence derived from studies of single cases reported to social service agencies; from studies with small, non-representative samples; from studies with low response rates; and from studies based on recall and the use of retrospective data. The authors conclude that it is difficult to understand the growing lobby for policies and programs to "deal with the problem" when there is such a lack of reliable knowledge about the incidence and prevalence, and when, in fact, relatively low rates have been reported.

Chapter 2 reviews the theoretical perspectives that have been used to explain elder abuse and neglect, including the child abuse and spouse abuse models, and three family violence approaches — the situational model, the social exchange perspective, and the symbolic interactionist perspective. After reviewing eight types of hypothesized individual, structural, or institutional factors associated with elder abuse and neglect, the authors, not surprisingly, conclude that no single theoretical perspective is likely to account for the occurrence or outcome of various events identified as elder abuse or neglect.

In Chapters 3 and 4, existing laws, legislation, and social services designed for the protection of vulnerable adults are presented and critiqued. Specifically, Chapter 3 discusses the pros and cons of guardianship laws (which are underdeveloped in Canada), while Chapter 4 reviews the types of intervention and mandated powers included in special adult protection legislation. This chapter also addresses the issue of mandatory reporting of observed incidents of abuse. The authors conclude that existing laws are of limited use in responding to the problem of elder abuse and neglect. Consequently, they stress that future laws and legislation must pay special attention to the rights of due process, and to individual rights of privacy and freedom as stated in sections 7 and 15(1) of the 1982 *Canadian Charter of Rights and Freedoms*.

The next two chapters focus on the application of existing policies, programs, and services. In Chapter 5, the authors present the pros and cons of three models or types of programs for successful intervention (adult protection, domestic violence, and advocacy). On the basis of a review of three major evaluation studies of abuse intervention programs, they stress the potential of the advocacy approach. Chapter 6 critically reviews the problems, guidelines, and devices for the screening of high-risk adults, for the assessment of the actual occurrence of neglect or abuse, and for the introduction of intervention protocols when abuse is identified. Practitioners are cautioned against adopting and using an assessment instrument or intervention protocol without evaluating whether there is valid and reliable evidence to justify its use in a practice setting. The authors stress that since much of the literature is theoretically and empirically clouded with doubt and uncertainty, the too-ready adoption of new devices or protocols may be potentially harmful to the recipient of such an intervention. As in previous monographs in this Series, the final chapter introduces policy options and issues, as well as immediate research needs, that must be addressed by policy makers and the research community.

In conclusion, like drug abuse and misuse, we know far less about the incidence and prevalence of elder abuse and neglect than we think we do. We know even less about why it occurs, under what circumstances, and how to prevent or alleviate such incidents. However, our understanding and our level of awareness are significantly enhanced by this thorough and critical review of the research literature, legislation, policies, and intervention services. Elder abuse and neglect are not the major concern or responsibility of one profession or one individual. Rather, all of those involved — older adults; practitioners and policy makers in the political, legal, health, and social welfare domains; children of older adults; gerontology students and practitioners; and the research community — must address the issues, questions, and concerns raised in this monograph. Effective programs, policies, and legislation to prevent abuse or neglect, to ensure compliance with existing laws and legislation, and to educate abusers and the abused can only be effectively designed and implemented if valid and reliable knowledge is both produced and widely disseminated. Thus, the challenge that lies ahead for the 1990s is to build on the present meagre research, policy, and practice base so that elder abuse and neglect will cease to be an "issue" or concern as we enter the twenty-first century.

Barry D. McPherson, Ph.D.
Series Editor
Wilfrid Laurier University
Waterloo, Ontario, Canada
January 1991

PREFACE

The intent of this monograph is to pause and take stock of the current state of affairs in the field of elder abuse and neglect. In this capacity our aims are threefold. As is the case with most issues in gerontology, the issue of elder abuse and neglect is a complicated problem requiring multi-disciplinary attention. Thus, this monograph represents an attempt to link the social, the legal, and the practice dimensions of elder abuse and neglect. For example, it is difficult to address legal issues without knowing the social parameters of the problem of abuse or to design legal remedies without the availability of supporting programs and practitioners to deliver services. Second, we critically evaluate the social and legal remedies available to Canadians from the vantage point of the existing research. Should there be mandatory or voluntary reporting of elder abuse? Are new programs and services required or should the existing programs and services be augmented? Should the abuser be the target of intervention along with the abused? Our final aim is to underscore the urgency for further research by identifying the theoretical and methodological flaws in the extant literature and by identifying issues that merit immediate study in order to advance our knowledge about elder maltreatment.

Chapter 1 begins with a review of current social and legal definitions of abuse, a description of the characteristics of the victims and the abusers, and a review of the studies regarding the incidence and the prevalence of elder abuse and neglect. Chapter 2 considers existing theoretical explanations of elder abuse and those factors known to be associated with the maltreatment of older adults. Chapter 3 details the existing legal solutions to elder abuse, and Chapter 4 critically examines special adult protection legislation. In Chapter 5, programs and services available for elderly persons who have been abused are reviewed and evaluated. Chapter 6 presents an overview of the state of direct practice and assesses the diagnostic, intervention, and preventative protocols offered to the practitioner. Chapter 7 concludes with a proposed agenda for research and directions for policy and practice that appear warranted in Canada.

As Canadians are poised to "do something" about elder abuse and neglect, it is hoped that this monograph will inform the debate about future courses of action in such a way that all older Canadians are assured health and dignity in their later years. The monograph should, therefore, be of interest to students of family violence and gerontology, to scholars, to practitioners, and to those who create laws and write policy.

ACKNOWLEDGEMENTS

Completion of *Elder Abuse and Neglect in Canada* would not have been possible without the co-operation and support of a number of organizations and individuals. Specifically, we wish to thank the Ontario Ministry of Community and Social Services for supporting the research upon which this volume is based. Additional support was received from the Canadian Research Institute for Law and the Family, funded by the Alberta Law Foundation, and the Faculty of Social Work, The University of Calgary.

We would also like to thank the many individuals who assisted in preparing this volume. John Wilson, Stan Loo, and Linda Perlis of the Ontario Ministry of Community and Social Services provided support and guidance in conducting the basic research for the work. Thanks are also due to Joanne Paetsch and Doreen Neville for their meticulous preparation of the manuscript.

We are especially grateful for the help of Barry McPherson, Series Editor; Sandra Magico, Acquisitions Editor and Marie Graham, Managing Editor, Legal and Academic Texts, both from Butterworths; to our Editor, Julia Keeler; and our anonymous reviewers, whose comments were invaluable.

CONTENTS

CHAPTER 1

THE DEFINITION, CONTEXT, AND PREVALENCE OF ELDER ABUSE AND NEGLECT

INTRODUCTION

Without doubt, the majority of older Canadians enjoy positive relationships with their families, friends, and relatives, and if institutionalized, with their professional caregivers. Nevertheless, there is a growing awareness that some elderly Canadians suffer abuse at the hands of these groups. Sensitization to this "new" form of violence has generated public, professional, and political concern, and concomitant pressure to ameliorate the problem. The demand for legal and social remedies has, however, outpaced the creation of cohesive policies to combat the problem as well as the research required to inform these policies. In fact, elder abuse, as a topic of research and policy formulation, has had an abbreviated history — a decade at most.

There is little consensus about what constitutes elder abuse and neglect, and as a result, estimates of the incidence and prevalence of the problem in Canada are imprecise at best. Furthermore, while 1 to 4 percent of elderly Canadians are reportedly abused, many researchers and practitioners hold that these figures represent the tip of the iceberg. In the light of the aging of the Canadian population, the reality of longer life spans, and the changing configuration of the family structure, elder abuse and neglect are predicted to increase. Theories to explain elder abuse are embryonic in nature and, for the most part, have been hastily borrowed from the field of child welfare and family violence. Few conceptual models for service delivery have been developed, and evaluation is rare. There are serious gaps in the research literature of specific interventions that can produce favourable outcomes for older persons, their families, and their formal caregivers. At the same time, what is known is not readily available to researchers, planners, and practitioners.

The dangers of developing both legal and social responses to elder abuse in the absence of knowledge are substantial. For example, mandatory reporting of elder abuse can constitute an infringement on the rights of older persons. In the name of protection, older persons can be forced to

1

accept services they do not desire, family relations can be severely strained and in some instances, the older adult can be institutionalized. The potential for "blaming the victim" should be readily apparent. As two Canadian experts have noted, "We, in Canada, know little about the phenomena of elder abuse and have no agreement about how to define it but we have strong 'gut feelings' that impel us to take some action. . . . We caution about undue haste" (Moore and Thompson 1987, 121).

Heeding the cautionary note struck by Moore and Thompson (1987), in this chapter we present the social and legal definitions of elder abuse and neglect and the social context in which they occur. The major definitional prolems are identified and the contradictory findings pertaining to the victim, the abuser, and the reporter are noted with an eye to laying the groundwork for the theme of this monograph — policy, programs, and practices in Canada are being erected on an insufficient theoretical and research foundation.

The first task in responding to and resolving any social problem is to identify the problem accurately and in a manner that can be understood by all who may have to deal with it. Unfortunately, the research and practice literature does not contain clear definitions of elder neglect and elder abuse. Indeed, if there is one recurring theme in the literature, it is the problem of adequately defining these terms — a serious matter, since the problems with definition ultimately translate into a variety of difficulties for the researcher, the policy maker, and the practitioner.

It has been argued that the terms *elder abuse* and *elder neglect* developed as folk categories. The labels evolved through use by those people directly exposed to the manifest reality of elder abuse who considered it important enough to warrant some type of classification (Sprey and Matthews 1989, 55). The outcome of this process has been a dearth of conceptual definitions of elder abuse and neglect, namely, definitions that detail the crucial attributes of the concepts and that help to distinguish the concepts from other concepts. Instead, most definitions are often clouded by vagueness, circularity, and a failure to distinguish between related concepts. Frequently, definitions will appear as typologies of behavioural manifestations, or conceptual definitions will be mixed with behavioural typologies (Hudson 1989, 7). For example, when there is no basis upon which to determine whether a behavioural manifestation is neglectful or abusive, how does one evaluate the family who lock up their confused and screaming mother for days on end?

While it has become almost fashionable to detail the definitional problems of abuse and neglect, doing so is a necessary step to understanding the current Canadian attempts to solve the problem and the surrounding issues. Policy based on faulty definitions of elder abuse and neglect can create an illusory sense of progress towards the solution of the problem; practitioners, attempting to meet the prescribed mandates of policy, may find the complexities of practice are not served; and older persons, who are the intended beneficiaries of such actions, may find their interests are not met.

RESEARCH DEFINITIONS OF ELDER ABUSE AND NEGLECT

In reviewing the research definitions of elder abuse and neglect it is important to note that researchers have focused exclusively on abuse perpetrated by caregivers. Further, little research has been undertaken to examine abuse and neglect of the elderly that takes place in institutional settings, such as hospitals and nursing homes. Offences committed by non-caregivers who are not family members are usually considered criminal acts and are classified as victimization rather than abuse. Thus, this review focuses exclusively on abuse perpetrated by caregivers and/or family members, usually in the domestic setting.

Within the above context, most social researchers have differentiated between physical abuse and psychological or verbal/emotional abuse in defining elder abuse (Lau and Kosberg 1979; O'Malley et al. 1979; Douglass et al. 1980; Crouse et al. 1981; Wolf et al. 1982; Giordano and Giordano 1984; Phillips and Rempusheski 1985; Podnieks et al. 1989). Neglect has also been included by many authors (O'Malley et al. 1979; McLaughlin et al. 1980; Hageboeck and Brandt 1981; Gioglio and Blakemore 1983; Hall and Andrew 1984; O'Brien et al. 1984). Other authors have differentiated between active and passive neglect (Douglass et al. 1980; Crouse et al. 1981; Wolf et al. 1982). Still others have added self-abuse and self-neglect to the concept of elder abuse (Hall and Andrew 1984; O'Brien et al. 1984). The end result is that dissimilar phenomena have been subsumed under the concept of elder abuse.

The literature also reveals that many authors have applied different terms to similar concepts. For example, exploitation (Lau and Kosberg 1979; O'Malley et al. 1979; Hall and Andrew 1984; O'Brien et al. 1984), financial abuse (Hageboeck and Brandt 1981; Gioglio and Blakemore 1983; Giordano and Giordano 1984), and material abuse (Wolf et al. 1982; Hall and Andrew 1984; Phillips and Rempusheski 1985) often refer to the same type of elder abuse.

Hudson and Johnson (1986) reviewed 31 empirical studies on elder abuse and found that physical and psychological abuse are uniformly included in definitions of elder abuse. However, distinctions between active and passive neglect and separate classifications of financial, material, or economic abuse, medical abuse, exploitation, violation of rights, self-neglect, and self-abuse vary from study to study.

The lack of a uniform and precise definition of elder abuse has resulted in contradictory reports of the incidence of elder abuse. For example, some authors have found that physical abuse is the most common form of elder abuse (Lau and Kosberg 1979; O'Malley et al. 1979; McLaughlin et al.

1980; Pepper and Oakar 1981), while others have found psychological abuse to be most prevalent (Boydston and McNairn 1981; Sengstock and Liang 1982; Wolf et al. 1982; Pratt et al. 1983). Douglass et al. (1980) and Crouse et al. (1981) found that passive neglect was most frequently reported in their studies, while several other researchers have claimed that financial abuse is the most common form of elder abuse (Shell 1982; Gioglio and Blakemore 1983; Podnieks et al. 1989).

Lastly, the paucity of precise definitions of the different types of elder abuse and neglect and the subsequent lack of accurate predictive criteria have made it difficult for both practitioners and the general public to identify cases of elder abuse and neglect (Phillips and Rempusheski 1986). It has been suggested that "research on the causes of abuse and neglect rather than on the symptoms can assist in the identification of at-risk persons and in the development of preventive programs" (M.F. Hudson 1986, 161).

A number of methods, ranging from formal protocols to general guidelines, have been proposed for detecting elder abuse (Fulmer 1982; O'Malley et al. 1983). These methods are reviewed in Chapter 5. However, in order for these tools to be useful, some consensus about the definitions of elder abuse and neglect is necessary so that standardized identification and detection procedures can be established (Hudson and Johnson 1986).

A Taxonomy of Elder Abuse

The first step in developing a comprehensive and useful definition is to develop a taxonomy of the various subcomponents or specific types included in the concept. The work of Wolf et al. (1982) provides the basis for a realistic taxonomy of the different types of abuse and neglect and is provided as an example in Table 1. These researchers divided elder abuse into three types: (1) physical abuse; (2) psychological abuse; and (3) material abuse. Elder neglect is divided into two major categories: (1) active neglect; and (2) passive neglect. For the most part, this framework is adopted in Table 1; however, active and passive neglect are categorized as intentional and unintentional neglect, since intention is an important dimension, and neglect by definition tends to be passive.

Physical abuse of the elderly receives the most attention in the literature and is the most easily identified category of elder abuse. Physical abuse refers to acts of commission that involve the intentional infliction of physical discomfort, pain, or injury (e.g., slapping, cutting, burning, physical coercion, or restraint, etc.) and that lead to bodily harm to the aged individual (Lau and Kosberg 1979; Douglass and Hickey 1983; O'Malley et al. 1983; Phillips and Rempusheski 1985; Valentine and Cash 1986; Wolf 1986). Physical abuse could also consist of medical maltreatment or sexual assault.

TABLE 1
SUMMARY OF RESEARCH DEFINITIONS OF ELDER ABUSE AND NEGLECT*

	Abuse		Neglect	
Physical	Psychological	Material	Intentional	Unintentional
• physical assault (e.g., hitting, slapping, pushing, etc.) • sexual assault • medical maltreatment • physical restraint • physical coercion	• verbal and non-verbal abuse • name calling and ignoring • emotional abuse • emotional deprivation • mental cruelty • threatening and frightening elder • provocation of fear • infantilization • humiliation • intimidation • isolation	• financial abuse • economic abuse • exploitation • misuse of money and property • theft of money and property • fraud	Intentionally or non-accidentally withholding: • physical requirements (e.g., medicine, food, clothing, housing, environmental, etc.) • psychological requirements (e.g., social contact, emotional support, respect, etc.)	Unintentionally or accidentally withholding: • physical requirements (e.g., medicine, food, clothing, housing, environmental) • psychological requirements (e.g., social contact, emotional support, respect)

* Self-abuse and self-neglect are also referred-to in the literature. However, they do not involve perpetrators and thus do not clearly fit in this paradigm.

SOURCE: J. Hornick, L. McDonald, G. Robertson, J.E. Wallace, *A Review of the Social and Legal Issues Concerning Elder Abuse* (Calgary, Alta.: Canadian Research Institute for Law and the Family, 1988).

Psychological abuse of the elderly is sometimes referred to as verbal or emotional abuse (Douglass et al. 1980; Crouse et al. 1981). This form of abuse involves the caregiver's intentional infliction of mental anguish or provocation of fear of violence or isolation in the elderly person. Such abuse may include verbal assaults upon the elderly (e.g., name-calling), humiliation or intimidation, threats of placement in a nursing home or isolation, or treatment of the elderly person as a child (Lau and Kosberg 1979; O'Malley et al. 1983; Giordano and Giordano 1984; Phillips and Rempusheski 1985; Valentine and Cash 1986; Wolf 1986). The category of psychological abuse has received considerable criticism because it includes all manner of family problems under the label of abuse (Callahan 1982; Pedrick-Cornell and Gelles 1982; Crystal 1986).

Since the concept of psychological abuse has been particularly difficult to define and measure, Podnieks et al. (1989) have concluded that it is more useful to concentrate on the major manifestations of psychological abuse, such as repeated insults or threats. Thus, they have identified an additional concept of "chronic verbal aggression."

Material abuse of the elderly is characterized by the intentional, illegal, or improper exploitation of the older person's material property or financial resources. Theft, conversion of money, or use of funds without the elderly person's authority or consent may be involved (Shell 1982; Douglass and Hickey 1983; Phillips and Rempusheski 1985; Stevenson 1985; Valentine and Cash 1986; Wolf 1986). Recently, Podnieks et al. (1989) operationalized material abuse more broadly as attempts to persuade or influence the elderly person to give up money and/or relinquish control over finances. Such broad definitions are more likely to measure the potential for this type of abuse rather than the abuse itself if it is assumed that the intent must be carried out, that is, exploitation must actually occur in order to be classified as "abuse."

In contrast to abuse, which is primarily active in nature, neglect is passive in nature and can be divided into intentional and unintentional neglect. Intentional neglect refers to the conscious failure to fulfil a caretaking obligation. Intentional neglect refers to those situations in which a caregiver knowingly impinges on the elderly person's well-being by limiting or denying the fulfilment of basic needs (Crouse et al. 1981; Wolf et al. 1982; Block 1983; Valentine and Cash 1986). This may include, for example, deliberate abandonment or deliberate denial of basic life essentials, such as food, water, clothing, or shelter, as well as social contact or emotional support.

Unintentional neglect refers to the failure to fulfil a caretaking obligation, *excluding* a conscious and intentional attempt to inflict physical or emotional stress on the elder. It includes situations in which the needs of the elder are unknown, are not fully recognized, or are not dealt with appropriately by the caregiver (Crouse et al. 1981; Wolf et al. 1982; Block 1983; Valentine and Cash 1986). Unintentional neglect often characterizes situations in which the caregiver has insufficient time, energy, or financial resources, or has inadequate knowledge or skills to provide proper care for the elderly person. Situations such as these may result in the lack of provision of food or health-related services, or in the elderly person's being left alone, forgotten, or isolated (Douglass and Hickey 1983; Wolf 1986; Podnieks 1988).

It is important to note again at this point that the social research definitions of elder abuse and neglect provided above involve either acts of commission or omission *on the part of the caregiver*, who is often a person the older person loves, trusts, and is dependent upon for care and assistance. This limits the concept of elder abuse to acts involving caregivers and serves to distinguish elder abuse and neglect from criminal acts against the elderly that occur in a broader context. Acts such as physical assault, rape, and burglary committed by someone other than a caregiver would not normally be considered elder abuse, although they do involve victimizing the elderly. In contrast, abuse may occur without the commission of a criminal act. For example, an elderly woman may willingly turn over all her pension cheques to a family member in return for a minimal level of care. If her action is voluntary, receiving the pension cheque would not constitute a criminal act, even though it could be exploitive.

In general, elder abuse and neglect may originate from two types of caregivers: (1) informal caregivers; and (2) formal caregivers. Both of these are briefly discussed below. Informal caregivers include family members or close familial associates. Since the vast majority of elderly persons live in their own homes or in the homes of relatives (Connidis 1989; Podnieks et al. 1989), abuse by informal caregivers, often referred to as familial or domestic abuse, is the most common type of abuse (M.F. Hudson 1986).

Formal caregivers include professionals who work with the elderly in a variety of settings. Nurses, physicians, and home care providers, for example, are formal caregivers. Elder abuse and neglect by professional or formal caregivers and abuse and neglect in institutional settings have only been recently addressed in the literature (Halamandaris 1983; Podnieks 1983; Solomon 1983).

Elder abuse and neglect by formal caregivers may fall into the same categories as those committed by informal caregivers (e.g., physical, psychological, and material abuse, intentional and unintentional neglect). The few articles addressing elder abuse and neglect in institutional settings tend to focus on material abuse, such as theft of patients' funds, medical care abuses (e.g., supplementing medical care support, charging costs unrelated to patient care, collecting for deceased or discharged patients, etc.), and fraudulent therapy and pharmaceutical charges (Halamandaris 1983; Pepper 1983; Stathopoulos 1983). The extent of these problems in Canada is unknown because there have been no studies of institutional abuse to date other than the reporting of anecdotal information (Goldstein and Blank 1988; Podnieks 1983).

It is also important to note at this juncture that caregiver abuse is not the whole story. There appears to be a category of independent elderly persons who are physically, psychologically, or financially abused by family members who are not caregivers (Pillemer and Finkelhor 1988; 1989). That is, relatively well-functioning older persons, who may have some responsibility for other relatives or who may have to interact with other relatives, are abused. Whether this is simply a matter of family violence (spouse abuse) or another unique manifestation of elder abuse remains to be debated.

Another type of abuse that does not seem to fit the taxonomy presented in Table 1 is self-abuse by an elderly person. This type of abuse refers to self-inflicted acts of commission that may result in physical, psychological, or material injury. Self-neglect also refers to acts of omission, such

as failure to take care of one's personal needs, which may result in physical or psychological injury (Hall and Andrew 1984; O'Brien et al. 1984;
Valentine and Cash 1986). Self-abuse and self-neglect often stem from
elderly persons' diminished physical or mental capabilities to care for
themselves (Giordano and Giordano 1984).

Although self-abuse and self-neglect have been referred to throughout
the literature as specific types of elder abuse and neglect, they do not
clearly fit into the typology outlined in Table 1. Quinn and Tomita suggest that "there is some question as to whether self-neglect and self-abuse
should be included when considering elder abuse and neglect" (1986,
52). Although self-abuse may take the form of physical, psychological,
or material abuse, and self-neglect may be either active or passive, they
do not clearly fit the paradigm, since there are no abusive caretakers
involved (Valentine and Cash 1986).

In such cases, older adults are generally considered responsible for caring for themselves unless they are found incapable or incompetent in a
court of law. Consequently, if they neglect or abuse themselves, it is seen
as a matter of free will. Issues arise regarding maintaining a balance
between the rights of individuals to autonomy, self-direction, and self-
determination and the protection of adults who are legally incompetent
to care for themselves (Valentine and Cash 1986). While it is clear that
protective services should investigate situations in which individuals are
placing themselves at risk, it remains unclear whether self-abuse and self-
neglect should be classified as types of elder abuse.

The Legal Definition of Elder Abuse

In comparison with the social research definitions, the legal definitions
of elder abuse are broader in scope. This is the case because legal definitions are linked to criminal law and prosecution in the criminal justice
system. However, legislative definitions are also problematic. If too
general a definition is adopted, there is a danger that the legislative
response will constitute unnecessary and unjustified intervention (Regan
1981; Faulkner 1982; Metcalf 1986). Moreover, as Katz notes:

> [T]he sweep of some of the definitions is tantamount to legislating against
> unkindness to the elderly. It must be borne in mind that "unreasonable
> or unrealistic laws serve neither the profession nor the public" [1980, 714–15]

Definitions of *abuse, neglect,* and *exploitation* vary significantly in the United
States (Lee 1986; Metcalf 1986). Physical injury is always included in the
definition of abuse, but only some states recognize the concept of emotional abuse (Metcalf 1986). This may reflect the problems associated with
defining and identifying emotional harm, as has been seen in the context of child welfare legislation (Katz 1980; Sharpe 1988). The U.S. legislation is most uniform in its definition of exploitation, which is generally

defined as the illegal or inappropriate use of another's resources for one's own profit or advantage (Lee 1986; Metcalf 1986).

Some American jurisdictions have adopted a narrow definition of abuse. For example, the Minnesota legislation defines it as the intentional and non-therapeutic infliction of physical pain or injury, or any persistent course of conduct intended to produce mental or emotional distress (Ontario Ministry of the Attorney General 1987). Likewise, the legislation in the District of Columbia, introduced in 1984, defines abuse in the following way:

a) The intentional or reckless infliction of serious physical pain or injury;

b) The use or threatened use of violence to force participation in sexual conduct;

c) The repeated, intentional imposition of unreasonable confinement, resulting in severe mental distress;

d) The repeated use of threats or violence, resulting in shock or an intense, expressed fear for one's life or of serious physical injury; or

e) The intentional or deliberately indifferent deprivation of essential food, shelter, or health care in violation of a caregiver's responsibilities, when that deprivation constitutes a serious threat to one's life or physical health. (Lewis 1986)

According to Lewis, the decision to restrict the definition to cases of serious injury was taken so as to avoid duplication of efforts. It was thought that existing services were adequate to deal with minor cases and that the protective services legislation (particularly in view of its mandatory reporting requirement) should be limited to cases of serious injury, with a further limitation that certain types of abuse be restricted to repeated occurrences.

In Canada, abuse is not defined concisely in the legislation. The Nova Scotia (1985) and New Brunswick (1980) statutes merely refer to adults who are victims of "physical abuse, sexual abuse, mental cruelty, or any combination thereof" (Gordon et al. 1986; Robertson 1987). The Newfoundland (1973) statute is directed only at "neglected" adults, but is probably broad enough to include cases of abuse. None of the statutes make express reference to financial abuse.

Unlike existing Canadian adult protection legislation, the new law in Prince Edward Island (*Adult Protection Act*, S.P.E.I. 1988, c. 6) provides a detailed definition in section (1) of abuse and neglect:

(a) "abuse" means offensive mistreatment, whether physical, sexual, mental, emotional, material or any combination thereof, that causes or is reasonably likely to cause the victim severe physical or psychological harm or significant material loss to his estate;. . .

(k) "neglect" means a lack of or failure to provide necessary care, aid, guidance or attention which causes or is reasonably likely to cause the victim severe physical or psychological harm or significant material loss to his estate.

It is significant that, like those in more recent enactments in the United States (such as the District of Columbia), these definitions restrict the scope of the proposed legislation to cases of serious harm. Unlike the definitions in existing Maritime legislation, they also include financial abuse.

SOCIAL CONTEXT OF ELDER ABUSE AND NEGLECT

This section refers primarily to incidents of elder abuse and neglect that occur in domestic settings and are committed by informal caregivers. Like other aspects of elder abuse and neglect, the characteristics of the victims and the perpetrators involved in abusive situations in institutional settings have been the subject of little research.

Characteristics of Victims

Several studies have reported that there appear to be distinct profiles of victims for different types of abuse (Phillips 1983; Giordano and Giordano 1984; Hudson and Johnson 1986; Wolf 1986; Bristowe and Collins 1989). Most of these studies, however, have not controlled for the type of abuse but rather focus on characteristics alone. The most commonly cited characteristics include: (1) age; (2) sex; and (3) disabilities and dependencies.

Age

Research findings indicate that most victims of elder abuse and neglect are the very old. That is, they are likely to be over 70 and, in most cases, between 75 and 85 years old (Rathbone-McCuan 1980; Steuer and Austin 1980; Boydston and McNairn 1981; Pepper and Oakar 1981; Sengstock and Liang 1982; Shell 1982; Rounds 1984; Podnieks 1985; Stevenson 1985; Sengstock and Barrett 1986; Wolf 1986; Hwalek 1988; Kosberg 1988; Podnieks 1989). It should be noted, however, that results vary among the studies. For example, O'Malley et al. (1979) found that victims were 75 years or older in 55 percent of the cases. Hwalek (1988) found that the age of victims ranged from 53 to 100 years and the average age was 77 years. In a recent study, however, Pillemer and Finkelhor (1988) found that the rates of abuse were no higher for older (i.e., over 75) than for younger (i.e., aged 65–74) elderly victims. And, in a recent Canadian study (Bristowe and Collins 1989), it was reported that victims of abuse (mean = 77) average only about five years younger than the average age of those housed in appropriate care settings (mean = 83).

Sex

It has been generally believed that most victims of elder abuse and neglect are female (Rathbone-McCuan 1980; Hageboeck and Brandt 1981; Wolf et al. 1982; Rounds 1984; Sengstock and Barrett 1986; Kosberg 1988; Mastrocola-Morris 1989; Podnieks 1989). For example, a number of studies have reported that as many as 70 to 80 percent of elder abuse victims are female (Lau and Kosberg 1979; O'Malley et al. 1979; Steuer and Austin 1980; Boydston and McNairn 1981; Sengstock and Liang 1982; Gioglio and Blakemore 1983; Podnieks 1985; Stevenson 1985; Hwalek 1988).

More recently it has been found that these findings may be misleading. For example, a study conducted in British Columbia (Bristowe and Collins 1989) reported that 72 percent of the victims are female. However, the authors also reported that 74 percent of their sample who were receiving appropriate care (i.e., non-victims) were also women. Even more controversial findings were reported by Pillemer and Finkelhor (1988). They found roughly equal numbers of abused elderly men and women (52 percent and 48 percent respectively). Furthermore, they suggested that the risk of abuse for elderly men is twice as much as that for elderly women (e.g., 51 per 1,000 versus 23 per 1,000), since fewer men constitute the elderly population than women. However, they also noted that abuse against elderly men seems to be less chronic and severe than abuse against women. Consistent with these findings, a cross-Canada prevalence study by Podnieks et al. found that females tended to be physically abused more than males (64 percent compared to 36 percent) (1989, 9).

Disabilities and Dependencies

In many abusive situations, the elderly person has physical and/or mental disabilities characterized as contributing to their dependence on their caregivers (Douglass et al. 1980; McLaughlin et al. 1980; Rathbone-McCuan 1980; Steuer and Austin 1980; Hageboeck and Brandt 1981; Podnieks 1985; Wolf 1986; Kosberg 1988; Podnieks 1989). Studies that have examined this particular aspect of the elderly victim have found that at least 75 percent usually have at least one major mental or physical impairment (Lau and Kosberg 1979; O'Malley et al. 1979; Boydston and McNairn 1981; Gioglio and Blakemore 1983). In a recent Canadian study (Bristowe and Collins 1989), it was reported that victims of abuse suffer less from confusion (e.g., 46 percent versus 73 percent) but more from depression (93 percent versus 70 percent) than elderly persons in non-abusive settings.

The most common physical problems of the elderly that may limit their activities include arthritis, heart conditions, rheumatism, hypertension, and impairments of the lower extremities, hips, back, and spine. In addition to physical problems, older persons are often functionally hampered by depression and organic brain syndromes, specifically delirium and dementia (Quinn and Tomita 1986).

Characteristics of Abusers

Some studies have suggested that there appear to be distinct profiles of abusers for different types of abuse (Phillips 1983; Giordano and Giordano 1984; Hudson and Johnson 1986; Wolf 1986; Kosberg 1988). However, most studies focus on the attributes and characteristics of abusive, informal caregivers regardless of the type of abuse. The most commonly reported characteristics include: (1) age; (2) sex; (3) relation to victim; (4) residence; and (5) substance abuse.

Age

Gioglio and Blakemore (1983) reported in one study that the age range of abusive caregivers is between 16 and 69 years of age. In most cases, however, the caregiver is middle-aged or elderly, although usually younger than the abused person. For example, Bristowe and Collins's (1989) findings from British Columbia indicated that the average age of caregivers is 20 years less than that of the care recipients. It is interesting to note that this is true for both abusive and non-abusive caregivers. Several studies have reported that most abusive informal caregivers range from middle age to age 60 (Wolf et al. 1982; Reece et al. 1983; Bristowe and Collins 1989). However, studies have also indicated that 25 to 50 percent of abusive caregivers are 60 years of age or older (Wills and Walker 1981; Reece et al. 1983; Steinmetz 1983; Sengstock and Barrett 1986). It appears that, on average, abusive informal caregivers tend to be middle-aged or older.

Sex

Generally, it has been suggested that women are more likely than men to assume the caregiving role, and women are also more likely to provide a higher level of caregiving (Reece et al. 1983; Yaffe 1988). Consequently, one would expect the majority of abusers to be female. However, the findings regarding the sex of abusive caregivers are mixed. Some studies report that the majority of abusers are women (Goldstein et al. 1981; Reece et al. 1983; Steinmetz 1983; Sengstock and Barrett 1986). Others show that the majority of abusers are men (Pepper and Oakar 1981; Wolf et al. 1982; Gioglio and Blakemore 1983; Stevenson 1985). A recent Canadian study (Bristowe and Collins 1989) indicated that 69 percent of non-abusive caregivers are female, whereas only 34 percent of abusive caregivers are female. In addition, they reported that when abusers are male, they deliver considerably more physical abuse than either verbal abuse or neglect.

Relation to Victim

In terms of the relationship between the elderly victim and his or her abuser, it has been repeatedly shown that the victim and the abuser are usually related (Wolf et al. 1982; Gioglio and Blakemore 1983; Reece et al. 1983; Wolf 1986). For example, it has been reported that in more than 80 percent of the cases the abuser is related to his or her victim (Lau and Kosberg 1979; O'Malley et al. 1979; Goldstein et al. 1981; Pillemer and Finkelhor 1988). Gioglio and Blakemore (1983) reported that 60.9 percent of abusers were from victims' immediate family and 13.0 percent from their extended family.

In most cases, the relative is the son or daughter of the elderly victim. Abuse by the elder's spouse, however, is also common (Steuer and Austin 1980; Hageboeck and Brandt 1981; Wills and Walker 1981; Sengstock and Liang 1982; Reece et al. 1983). According to Phillips, "there is reason to believe that a certain proportion of elder abuse is actually spouse abuse grown old" (1986, 212). In addition, Giordano and Giordano (1984) reported that spouse abuse was a predominant variable in elder abuse.

In terms of Canadian studies, Bristowe and Collins (1989) reported that 44.8 percent of the abusive caregivers were spouses, 13.8 percent were daughters or daughters-in-law, and 13.8 percent were sons or sons-in-law. It is interesting to note that 37.8 percent of non-abusive caregivers were spouses, 43.2 percent were daughters or daughters-in-law, and 5.4 percent were sons or sons-in-law. The remaining 27.6 percent of abusive caregivers and 13.6 percent of non-abusive caregivers consisted of grand-children, neighbours, boarders, foster children, paid caregivers, or other non-specified caregivers.

A recent study by Podnieks et al. (1989) found that the relationship to the victim was associated with the type of abuse. Material abusers tended to be distant relatives or non-relatives who were not caretakers, while those who inflicted chronic verbal aggression and physical abuse tended to be spouses.

Residence

In most cases the abuser lives with the victim (McLaughlin et al. 1980; Boydston and McNairn 1981; Hageboeck and Brandt 1981; Pepper and Oakar 1981; Wolf et al. 1982; Sengstock and Barrett 1986; Pillemer and Finkelhor 1988). It has also been found that the abuser is frequently dependent on the elderly victim for financial support and housing (Wolf et al. 1982; Pillemer 1986; Kosberg 1988). Pillemer (1985a) found that 42.9 percent of abusive caretakers were entirely dependent and 11.9 percent were somewhat dependent on their victims for housing.

Substance Abuse

Substance abuse, primarily alcohol abuse, has been found to be prevalent among abusers of the elderly (Lau and Kosberg 1979; O'Malley et al. 1979; Rathbone-McCuan 1980; Pepper and Oakar 1981; Wolf et al. 1982; Giordano and Giordano 1984; Pillemer 1986; Chance 1987; Kosberg 1988). On the basis of their British Columbia study, Bristowe and Collins (1989) suggested that alcohol use is the most obvious difference between abusive and non-abusive caregivers. For example, they found that 88 percent of abusive caregivers reported alcohol use, compared to only 30 percent of non-abusive caregivers. However, it is important to note that these percentages for alcohol use reflect those who use alcohol at all — regardless of whether it is "socially," "occasionally," or "often or excessively." When alcohol consumption is greater (i.e., "often"), Bristowe and Collins found that physical and verbal abuse are likely consequences and abuse is more severe and more frequent. Research findings also indicate that many abusers have a history of psychological problems or mental illness (Wills and Walker 1981; Wolf et al. 1982; Kosberg 1988). Pillemer (1986) found that 79 percent of the abused elderly reported that their abusive caregivers had psychological or emotional problems compared to 24 percent of the non-abused elderly.

PREVALENCE OF ELDER ABUSE AND NEGLECT

During the past 50 years, major demographic changes have inadvertently brought attention to the general problems and concerns of older persons, as well as to the specific issue of elder abuse. For example, life expectancy for both men and women has continued to increase since 1931. For men, the life expectancy has risen from 60 years of age in 1931 (Foot 1982) to 71.9 years in 1980–82 (Statistics Canada 1984). Contrary to popular belief, the greatest gains in life expectancy have been made at the younger ages, especially in the first year of life (McDaniel 1986). Since the 1970s, infant mortality, which is considered to be a chief indicator of improved longevity, has continued to decline.

As a result of increased life expectancy and population growth increases in general, there are growing numbers of individuals who are 60 years old or older, and the aging of the population continues to accelerate. For example, in 1983 the median age of the Canadian population was 30 years of age. It is projected that by 2006 the median age will be 41 years and will reach 48 years by 2031 (Statistics Canada 1985). Not only has the number of individuals over 60 increased, but the proportion of the population over 60 has also increased. According to McDaniel, "it therefore seems realistic to anticipate that approximately one-quarter of Canada's population in fifty years' time will be comprised of people over the age of 65" (1986, 106). In actual numbers, this implies there will be 7 million older people in Canada by the first third of the twenty-first century (Statistics Canada 1985).

The increase in the proportion of the population 65 years of age and over has led many to conclude that, as a greater number of older persons become dependent on others for their care, there will be an increase in elder abuse (Montgomery and Borgatta 1986). This hypothesis is based on the assumption that living with or being responsible for chronically ill elderly persons is extremely taxing on members of the family, thus leading to the increased probability that abuse will occur.

Unfortunately, both the public and the scientific community have been all too willing to accept claims concerning the "explosion" of elder abuse as well as the "tip of the iceberg" theories carried over from the early development of research in the child abuse area. This had led to a rapid growth in the scientific literature concerned with detection, prevention, and intervention with the abused elderly — without reference to reliable statistics on the incidence or prevalence of elder abuse. Thus, as Montgomery and Borgatta (1986, 598) point out, "one could easily be led to believe that elder abuse exists, is growing, and that there is considerable knowledge about its causes and prevention."

The Limitations of Prevalence and Incidence Studies

Although numerous studies have been conducted that document the existence and nature of elder abuse and neglect, only a few studies have focused specifically on the prevalence (i.e., lifetime occurrence after 65 years of age) and/or the incidence (i.e., new occurrence within a specific time frame — usually one year) of elder abuse and neglect. To complicate matters further, many of the studies that report rates of occurrence of elder abuse are limited by methodological problems, including weak research designs, invalid instruments, low response rates, and nonrepresentative samples. These limitations, added to the conceptual and dysfunctional problems discussed earlier in this chapter, hamper the achievement of valid estimates of the incidence and prevalence of elder abuse.

Current estimates of the number and the incidence of elder abuse cases are often based on cases reported to social service agencies. Heavy reliance on this data source is problematic for a number of reasons: (1) agency figures represent an unknown fraction of the total number of actual cases; (2) reported cases most likely result in a biased representation of the most extreme and severe cases; (3) lack of uniformity of state and provincial reporting laws and record keeping affects the number of cases reported; (4) recency of the awareness regarding elder abuse and neglect results in a low level of awareness among professionals, the public, and even victims themselves; and (5) the number of cases reported to agencies varies by type of agency, title, location, etc. (Pedrick-Cornell and Gelles 1982; Giordano and Giordano 1984; Hudson and Johnson 1986).

The results of many studies are also based on small, non-representative samples (Pedrick-Cornell and Gelles 1982; Giordano and Giordano 1984; Moore and Thompson 1987; Bristowe and Collins 1989). For example, on the basis of a small, non-representative sample of 105 professionals in Manitoba, Shell generalized her findings in an unpublished but widely distributed report (1982), and estimated that 2.2 percent of 18,000 persons receiving care are abused by their caregivers. In another unpublished study, Block and Sinnott (1979) achieved a response rate of only 16.48 percent. According to Pedrick-Cornell and Gelles, "Regardless of how large their sample was, their estimate of national incidence is based on a total of *between 1 and 3 actual reports of elderly abuse*" (1982, 460).

In most studies, retrospective data are collected from professionals or experts in the field who have either direct contact with or firsthand knowledge of elder abuse victims. In these cases, researchers rely on the memory, attitudes, judgement, and impressions of the professional (M.F. Hudson 1986; Poertner 1986; Moore and Thompson 1987; Filinson 1989). Further, in most studies there is a lack of control for duplication of reporting of cases. As a result, cases may be counted more than once (M.F. Hudson 1986). If the possibility of duplication of cases is not taken into account, there is no way of determining whether the same case of elder abuse has been reported by two or more separate respondents (Moore and Thompson 1987).

Finally, it is impossible to know whether or not the rates have actually increased, since there is no accurate record of the amount of current or past abuse (Connidis 1989). Furthermore, most discussions of the changes in the amount of abuse fail to recognize the critical difference between absolute numbers, or incidence of abuse, and rates of abuse. For example, even if the rates of abuse remain the same, the absolute number of abused elders will increase because the number of elderly persons is growing. Thus, it is necessary to distinguish between absolute numbers and rates of elder abuse (Pillemer and Finkelhor 1988; Connidis 1989).

Given the general poor state of the research on the incidence and the prevalence of elder abuse and neglect, it is easy to mislead readers in presenting findings of studies. Thus, in the sections to follow only studies that meet rigorous scientific standards for incidence and prevalence are reviewed in detail.

Canadian Studies

To date, only one rigorous, comprehensive study of elder abuse has been conducted. This study, conducted by Podnieks et al. (1989), consisted of a cross-Canada telephone survey of 2,000 randomly chosen elderly persons living in private houses. The respondents were asked to provide information on whether they had been abused since the age of 65 years by family members, or other intimates, in the following four areas: (1) material abuse; (2) chronic verbal aggression; (3) physical violence; and (4) neglect. The results of the study indicated that material abuse was the most widespread form of maltreatment, with 2.5 percent (25 per 1,000) of the sample reporting that someone had tried to persuade, cheat, or influence them in relation to finances. Chronic verbal aggression was the second most common form of abuse, reported by 1.4 percent (14 per 1,000) of the sample. Physical violence was reported by 0.5 percent (5 per 1,000) of the respondents, and neglect was the least common form of maltreatment, with only 0.4 percent of the sample reporting it. Both physical abuse and chronic verbal aggression tended to be perpetrated by spouses, whereas material abuse (measuring potential rather than actual abuse) tended to be perpetrated by distant relatives or non-relatives. Overall findings indicated that about 4 percent (40 per 1,000) of the elderly population have experienced some form of maltreatment since they passed their 65th birthday.

American Studies

Two rigorous American studies have attempted to identify the incidence of elder abuse. Gioglio and Blakemore (1983) interviewed a stratified, random sample of persons 65 years of age or older living in the community. On the basis of information collected from 342 respondents (88.3 percent response rate), their findings indicated that 1 percent of the respondents included in their survey were victims of some form of abuse. Financial abuse occurred in 50 percent of the cases, and physical abuse was the least reported form of maltreatment.

In a more recent study, Pillemer and Finkelhor (1988) conducted a large-scale stratified, random survey that involved telephone interviews with 2,020 community-dwelling elderly persons in Boston regarding their experience of physical and verbal abuse and neglect. They found that 63 elderly persons had been maltreated — an overall rate of mistreatment of 32 elderly persons per 1,000, or 3.2 percent. More specifically, 40 persons experienced physical abuse (20 per 1,000); 26, verbal aggression (11 per 1,000); and 7, neglect (4 per 1,000).

The only rigorous study of abuse of patients in nursing homes has been carried out in the United States. Pillemer and Moore (1989) conducted a random survey of 577 nurses and nursing home aides working in long-term care facilities. Staff were asked to report on abuse perpetrated by others and to report on their own abusive actions. Only physical and psychological abuse were included in the study. The researchers found that, overall, 36 percent of the sample had seen at least one incident of physical abuse in the preceding year. The most frequent type of physical abuse observed by staff was excessively restraining a patient. A total of 81 percent of the respondents had witnessed at least one psychologically abusive incident in the preceding year. The most frequent type of psychological abuse observed by staff was yelling at a patient in anger (70 percent). Ten percent of the respondents reported that they themselves had committed one or more physically abusive acts, and 40 percent reported that they had committed at least one psychologically abusive act within the preceding year. The most common form of physical abuse was use of excessive restraints (6 percent) and the most common form of psychological abuse was yelling at a patient (33 percent).

CONCLUSIONS

The definitions of elder abuse found in the family violence and gerontological literature are generally vague and imprecise. However, certain trends emerged from a review of the social definitions of elder abuse. First, these definitions tended to focus on physical abuse and both active and passive neglect. Second, there was some clouding of the differences between abuse and neglect. Third, the social research seemed to concentrate mainly on abuse or neglect that occurred in the home or domestic setting and was perpetrated by informal caregivers who are in a position of trust and authority, such as spouses or other family members.

On the other hand, social definitions of elder abuse tended not to include material abuse or abuse of property. Likewise, these definitions seldom included abuse perpetrated by formal (i.e., professional) caregivers in an institutional setting or by family members who are not caregivers. Finally, self-abuse and self-neglect were usually considered to be distinct from elder abuse inflicted by a perpetrator.

The legal definitions of elder abuse in many American states are broader than the definitions used in social research, since they recognize physical abuse, neglect, and exploitation (material abuse). Furthermore, the legal definitions of abuse tend to focus on all perpetrators as opposed to just informal or formal caregivers. Definitions of neglect are more specific in the sense that they often identify the specific responsibilities of individual caregivers.

The major limitation of existing legal definitions of elder abuse in Canada (aside from the fact that many jurisdictions such as Nova Scotia do not define elder abuse at all) is that they are defined in the light of the *Criminal Code* or of specific provincial legislation and thus may limit prosecution to only the more serious cases.

Although some studies suggest that specific types of victims may be susceptible to specific types of abuse, most studies report that the ''typical'' victim of elder abuse is likely to be a 75- to 85-year-old woman, who is probably widowed or single, and of lower socio-economic class. She probably has physical and/or mental disabilities and, as a result, is highly dependent on her caregiver for her emotional and physical needs. Notwithstanding the contrary evidence that has recently come to light (Pillemer and Finkelhor 1988; Podnieks et al. 1989), the problem is that these descriptions do little to differentiate the abused and neglected from the rest of the older population. Most people over the age of 65 have at least one chronic illness or impairment, although most are not severely limited by it (Chappell et al. 1986). The preponderance of elders are women; in fact, the sex ratio for those 70 to 79 in Canada is 76 males per 100 females (Gee and Kimball 1987). Therefore, the profile of the elderly person who is a victim of abuse and neglect does not appear to differ significantly from the profile of the elderly person who is not a victim.

The findings regarding the perpetrators of elder abuse are also equivocal. Some studies have suggested that distinct types of perpetrators commit specific types of abuse. However, generally the abuser is reportedly a middle-aged married or single son or daughter of the victim. Abusive caregivers may experience a great deal of stress as a result of their overwhelming duties and are often characterized as substance abusers and/or persons with psychological problems.

It is important to note that the profiles of the abused and the abuser have limited utility given the heterogeneity of the elderly population. Because elder abuse is believed to cross ethnic, social, and socio-economic strata, it is difficult to distinguish profiles of the elderly who are involved in abusive situations from profiles of those who are not (J.E. Hudson 1986). In addition, studies have shown that a significant number of elder abuse victims do not fit the "typical" profile and that a significant number do fit the profile but are not abused (Quinn and Tomita 1986; Wolf 1986; Pillemer and Finkelhor 1988; Podnieks et al. 1989).

Although a number of studies have been conducted on the incidence of elder abuse in both Canada and the United States, the results of these studies can at best be considered only rough estimates because of the many definitions and the methodological problems associated with these studies. The lack of reliability of the findings seems to be a result of the following problems: (1) there has been a lack of consistency in the operational definition of elder abuse used in various studies; (2) no distinction has been made between incidence (new occurrence within a specific time frame — usually one year) and prevalence (lifetime occurrence — i.e., after 65 years of age); (3) incidence is often based on cases reported to social service agencies; (4) in survey studies, mainly small, non-representative samples have been used; (5) response rates in surveys have been inconsistent; (6) there has been wide use of retrospective data; and (7) there has been little or no attempt to control for duplication of cases.

The reliable studies available would suggest that the prevalence of elder abuse and neglect in Canada is about 4 percent. This figure is comparable to the estimate for the elderly American population identified by Gioglio and Blakemore (1983) and Pillemer and Finkelhor (1988), which is between 1 and 4 percent of the elderly population. One American study provides preliminary evidence for the physical and psychological abuse of nursing home patients; however, there are no extant Canadian studies about the incidence and the prevalence of elder abuse in institutions.

Given the lack of reliable knowledge in the area of incidence and prevalence of elder abuse and the relatively low rates identified, it is difficult to understand the lobby for policies and programs to deal with the problem. Unfortunately, as Montgomery and Borgatta (1986, 600) conclude:

> . . . it appears that the scientific community, rather than being the leader in generating accurate information, has been the follower in repeating inaccurate information and has gone on inappropriately to generate false statements.

CHAPTER 2

THEORETICAL EXPLANATIONS OF ELDER ABUSE AND NEGLECT

During the past 25 years a considerable amount of research has been conducted in the area of family violence. In the early 1960s, child abuse and neglect were unwillingly acknowledged, and in the 1970s spouse abuse was more readily recognized as a social problem that demanded immediate attention. Between 1977 and 1981, the existence of elder abuse and neglect was revealed when the Select Committee on Aging of the U.S. House of Representatives held public hearings on the topic (Douglass 1983). Thus, even though elder abuse and neglect are by no means new phenomena, they have only recently received public attention as serious social problems.

It has been observed in the literature that empirical evidence on elder abuse is scarce and that there is a corresponding lack of empirically generated and tested theoretical propositions on the causes of abuse and neglect of the elderly (Pedrick-Cornell and Gelles 1982; Pillemer 1986). There are only a few studies involving the testing of a multivariate explanatory model (Phillips 1983; Pillemer and Suitor 1988; Steinmetz 1988). Theoretical work on elder abuse has been drawn primarily from the theories and propositions developed and applied to other forms of intrafamilial violence, such as child abuse and spouse abuse (Block and Sinnott 1979; Pedrick-Cornell and Gelles 1982; Giordano and Giordano 1984).

Many of the elder abuse models copied the child abuse model, since several parallels can be drawn between the battered child and the battered parent. First, both are dependent on others to ensure that their basic needs are met. The elderly, like children, have been found to suffer from a "failure-to-thrive syndrome" and both may be incapable of asking for what they need to survive. Second, both are presumed to receive loving care and support from their caregivers. Third, both the dependent child and the dependent elderly person can be a source of extreme physical, emotional, and financial stress for the caregiver (Steinmetz 1978; Quinn and Tomita 1986).

However, there are several fundamental flaws in this parallel between child abuse and elder abuse. First, not all elder abuse involves a caregiver

21

abusing a dependent victim. Research has shown that in many cases the abuser is the dependent person, not the victim (Pillemer 1985a; Breckman and Adelman 1988). Second, in those cases where the elder is dependent, the dependency is quite different from that of a child. For example, parents clearly have a legal responsibility for children, whereas most caregivers to the elderly do not. This leads to serious problems associated with modelling policy and legislation for elder abuse on responses to child abuse. According to Douglass:

> The principal problem with modeling such children's service systems . . .
> is the independent, competent, adult status of most victims of abuse or
> neglect of the elderly in contrast to the minority status of children who are
> neglected or abused. [1983, 401]

The rights of elderly victims must not be compromised by well-intentioned systems that treat competent elderly victims as if they were children. For example, many current mandatory reporting laws and intervention procedures violate the rights and privileges of an otherwise independent adult and also override the confidentiality privileges of human service providers (Crystal 1987). In both spouse abuse and elder abuse, the victims are adults who are legally capable of making their own decisions unless a court of law rules otherwise and appoints a guardian or trustee (Quinn and Tomita 1986).

It has been argued that elder abuse has much more in common with spouse abuse than with child abuse (Breckman and Adelman 1988; Pillemer and Finkelhor 1988; Mastrocola-Morris 1989), since "there is reason to believe that a certain proportion of elder abuse is actually spouse abuse grown old" (Phillips 1986, 212). Elders are most likely to be abused by the person with whom they live, and many studies have found that elders live with their spouse. It is not suggested, however, that spouses are inherently more violent towards their partners than adult children are to their parents. Instead, Pillemer and Finkelhor suggest that:

> [B]ecause spouses are more likely to be present in an elderly person's house-
> hold, their opportunities for abusive behavior appear to be greater. If more
> elderly persons lived with their children, there would probably be more
> child-to-elder violence. [1988, 55]

Many women are subject to a lifetime of abuse that begins with physical and sexual abuse as children. Later in life they get married and find they are victims of spouse abuse, and as they grow older they become victims of elder abuse. Mastrocola-Morris (1989) refers to this as a "continuum of violence," which stretches from childhood through marriage, and finally into middle and old age. This raises an important issue of whether elder abuse is a unique category of family violence, or whether it is simply a modified category of another type of family violence that is distinguished by the age of the victim (Steinmetz 1988).

If elder abuse is treated as more closely related to spouse abuse than child abuse, ageist attitudes are avoided and it is more likely that older persons will be treated as independent, responsible adults. In addition, the comparison with battered women suggests that similar facilities, such as emergency shelters and safe houses, would be useful for victims of elder abuse. Lastly, using the spouse abuse analogy supports the use of criminal sanctions, which may prevent the revictimization of elderly persons, and also encourages the use of victim assistance programs for victims of elder abuse.

Regardless of the position taken about the similarities and differences between elder abuse and neglect, child abuse and neglect, and spouse abuse, it is important to note that the theories presented in the literature to date are limited to abuse occurring in domestic situations. Until now, only one theoretical work (Pillemer 1988) has attempted to explain elder abuse and neglect by formal caregivers in institutional settings. Pillemer presents a theoretical model of potential causes of patient maltreatment, including exogenous variables, nursing home environment, staff characteristics, and patient characteristics. However, J.E. Hudson suggests that:

> Although no satisfyingly comprehensive theory has appeared to explain institutional abuse, some of the hypotheses invoked to elucidate family mediated abuse seem equally applicable here. [1986, 18]

For example, she suggests that dependence factors, personality traits of the abuser, internal stressors, external stressors, and societal attitudes towards the elderly may also explain elder abuse and neglect by formal caregivers. Pillemer's proposed model (1988) seems consistent with Hudson's argument. Since at this time there is a dearth of research available in this area, it remains to be seen whether or not these factors contribute to elder abuse and neglect in institutional settings. Institutional factors hypothesized and found to be related to elder abuse and neglect by formal caregivers are also discussed briefly below.

THE STATE OF THE ART

Family Violence Approaches to Elder Abuse and Neglect

Much of the literature does not make the important distinction between theoretical explanations and causal factors related to elder abuse and neglect. For example, a theory provides a systematic explanation for observed facts in the form of interconnected propositions regarding the relations between specific variables or factors. However, in the literature, specific factors, such as stress and dependency, are often treated as theoretical explanations when these are merely factors that may be incorporated into one of a number of theories that attempt to explain elder abuse and neglect. The specific relationships between those factors and elder abuse form propositions upon which theories are built.

Several family violence approaches have been used in an attempt to explain elder abuse and neglect. The following theories have been identified: (1) the situational model; (2) social exchange theory; and (3) the symbolic interaction approach. While these three theories are neither mutually exclusive nor exhaustive, they provide a theoretical framework for the most widely discussed causal factors related to elder abuse and neglect.

Each of the three theoretical explanations incorporates a variety of causal factors that are also discussed below. Any one of these factors may be included in any one of the theoretical explanations. However, different theories tend to emphasize certain factors more than others. For example, the situational model emphasizes internal and external stressors, such as life crises and negative environmental conditions. The social exchange model stresses the importance of the web of dependencies and the personality traits of the abuser. In contrast, the symbolic interaction approach emphasizes the role of the transgenerational violence and filial crisis factors. It has been argued that these perspectives are competing explanations of elder abuse and neglect (Phillips 1986, 214), yet a review of the three theories would suggest that each attempts to explain different types of abuse and neglect.

The Situational Model

At this time, the most widely accepted explanatory approach for elder abuse is the situational model, which has been argued to have its roots in the child abuse and intrafamily violence literature (Phillips 1986, 198).

> The basic premise of the situational model is that as the stress associated with certain situational and/or structural factors increases for the abuser, the likelihood increases of abusive acts directed at a vulnerable individual who is seen as being associated with the stress. [Phillips 1986, 198]

This approach suggests that mistreatment is an irrational response to environmental conditions and situational life crises. In addition, according to this model, earlier development is less important than present situations and social conditions (Shell 1982).

The situational variables hypothesized to be associated with domestic elder abuse and neglect include: (1) caregiver-related factors; (2) elder-related factors; and (3) socio-structural factors. It should be noted that the factors related to these three variables are not necessarily mutually exclusive. For example, caregiver-related factors may result from transgenerational or learned violence, personality traits, web of dependencies, filial crisis, and internal stress. Elder-related factors tend to stem primarily from a web of dependencies, although they may also result from transgenerational violence or internal stress. Socio-structural factors may include external stressors and societal attitudes towards the elderly.

One major flaw of this perspective, besides the fact that it is poorly constructed, is that it fails to account for the fact that individuals experience similar situations and environmental crises but respond differently. This suggests that, although environmental factors are important, they are insufficient predictors of elder abuse and neglect (Shell 1982). This approach then, rather than predictive, is simply *ad hoc*, in that it can only delineate causal factors retrospectively after the incident has occurred.

Social Exchange Theory

Social exchange theory is based on the assumption that social interaction involves an exchange of rewards and punishments between at least two people, and that all individuals seek to maximize rewards and minimize punishments (Phillips 1986). In most relationships, all things are not equal, since individuals have different access to resources and different capabilities for providing instrumental services. According to the social exchange model, these imbalances form the basis of power.

The social exchange theory posits that as older people age they have less access to power, since they have fewer resources and are progressively less able to perform instrumental tasks. As aging progresses, the imbalance grows and the elderly generally become more powerless, dependent, and vulnerable than their caregivers, a process that Steinmetz (1983) calls, "generational inversion." This perspective focuses on the dependence and the vulnerable characteristics of the elderly in its explanation of elder abuse and neglect.

One problem with this approach is that the dependency sometimes operates in the opposite direction. In fact, Pillemer (1986) applies exchange theory to account for the dependency of relatives on the abused. That is, abuse could stem from the abuser's dependency and the sense of powerlessness of the abuser (Pillemer 1985a, 155). In addition, social exchange theory assumes that people are rational and will do something only in exchange for something else. Thus, this approach would not be useful for explaining abuse that is primarily the result of idiosyncratic personality traits or unexpected crisis situations.

The Symbolic Interaction Approach

Symbolic interaction is a process that involves at least two individuals. This process occurs over time, consists of identifiable phases that are recurring and interrelated, and requires constant negotiation and renegotiation. In this approach, which is tied to social learning and modelling, mistreatment is viewed as a recurring phenomenon within the family, a phenomenon that is cyclic in nature and is related to the family's history of violent relationships (Shell 1982).

> Elder abuse can be conceptualized as an inadequate or inappropriate role enactment arising from cognitive processes that alter role improvisation and role imputation for both the elder and the perpetrator. [Phillips 1986, 209]

According to Gelles (1979), the symbolic interaction approach to family violence examines the different meanings of violence that people hold and the consequences that these meanings have in certain situations. It suggests not only that abusers learn how to be violent from witnessing violence or suffering from violence, but also that victims learn to be more accepting of abuse.

In a direct application of the symbolic interaction model, Steinmetz in her inductive study of elder abuse discovered that "dependency stress," a subjective interpretation of the stress carried by the family caregiver, was twice as likely to predict feelings of burden compared with the actual level of dependency (1988, 218). Thus, this perspective should address the process involved in the construction of violence and the dynamics of the violent situation.

This model does not include all the variables helpful in explaining elder abuse. For example, it does not account for structural variables or processes that may influence the abusive situation. However, it does highlight several factors that need further attention, since they have been largely neglected by the literature. This model emphasizes the transgenerational violence and filial crisis factors.

IN SEARCH OF A THEORY

The development of a comprehensive and useful theory requires continual empirical testing and verification of propositions that are directly related to a model or a theory. The results of empirical testing not only provide useful descriptive information, but are also essential for refining or modifying aspects of a theory or a model.

As mentioned above, however, there is a notable lack of empirically generated and tested theoretical propositions regarding the causes of abuse and neglect of the elderly. The few studies that have attempted formally to test a theory have had such poor research designs that the validity of the results is seriously questioned. Furthermore, the evidence that has been presented does not provide overwhelming empirical support for one perspective over another. However, it seems that one perspective alone is not adequate to explain all of the different cases of the complex phenomenon of elder abuse. According to Phillips:

> No one theoretical base will provide a comprehensive, all inclusive explanation of elder abuse. . . . As a result, probably the best resolution to this controversy will be in efforts to integrate theoretical perspectives using those variables with the most explanatory power from any or all theories available. [1986, 214]

Interestingly enough, there has been little theoretical activity that draws upon theories in social gerontology (see Marshall 1987; McPherson 1990). While information on "caregiver stress" has been a source that has been mined, scant attention has been paid to such perspectives as generational solidarity, network theory, continuity theory, or political economy theory. All of these theories could possibly contribute to an understanding of different aspects of elder abuse. For example, the intergenerational solidarity framework provides a meaningful way of studying the family as a social support system. Six dimensions of intergenerational solidarity have been identified — family structure, associational solidarity, affective solidarity, functional solidarity, consensual solidarity, and normative solidarity (see Rosenthal 1987). When some of the elements are perceived to be low or negative, adult-child-to-elder abuse may be one of the outcomes. Continuity theory (see McPherson 1990) may have some bearing on the continuance of violence to the end of the life cycle. The social network approach (see Wellman and Hall 1984; Corin 1987) provides a composite picture of social ties and may have possibilities for predicting elder abuse and neglect. At the broader societal level, the political economy approaches to aging (see Estes et al. 1982) might have something to offer in explaining how and why elder abuse has become a social problem. There is little doubt that the definition of the phenomenon and its management have been influenced by social, political, and economic forces. Mandatory reporting in the United States would be an example of the outcome of political processes, while the lack of commitment of financial resources for service delivery (Callahan 1988) may reflect economic reality, or society's attitudes towards the aged.

CAUSAL FACTORS ASSOCIATED WITH ELDER ABUSE AND NEGLECT

Little research exists that has attempted to test any of the theories discussed above. Considerably more research has involved testing the relationships between specific factors and elder abuse and neglect, although without the contextual base of any particular theory. Therefore, more attention has been placed in this chapter on the discussion of the factors hypothesized to be related to elder abuse and neglect.

This section will review eight types of factors hypothesized to be associated with elder abuse and neglect: (1) transgenerational family violence; (2) web of dependencies; (3) personality traits of the abuser; (4) filial crisis; (5) internal and external stressors; (6) social isolation; (7) societal attitudes towards the elderly; and (8) institutional factors. Some of these factors seem to correspond to the theories discussed above. However, it should be noted that the explanatory power of these factors has only been tested in bivariate relationships and not as part of a theoretical model.

The review of these types of factors indicates that no single explanation has been developed to explain elder abuse and neglect. Instead, we have an array of various potential explanations of the phenomena. It should be noted that the causal factors presented below are not the only ones that could be included; however, they are the most widely examined in the literature and the existing research. Each type is discussed and the degree to which each factor has been found to be related to elder abuse and neglect is reported.

Transgenerational Family Violence

This factor is based on the assumption that "violence is a normative behavioral pattern which is learned in the context of the family" (Giordano and Giordano 1984, 234). Through observation and participation, children learn that violence is an acceptable response to stress. Pillemer (1986) refers to this as the intergenerational transmission of violent behaviour, in which a "cycle of violence" occurs from generation to generation. It has been suggested that children who were abused by their parents are more likely to be child abusers than those who were not abused. This transmision of violent behaviour may occur through the reinforcement of a subculture that accepts violence.

Straus et al. (1980) found that the greater the physical punishment received from one's parent, the higher the rate of abusive behaviour towards one's children. In addition, they found that children who observed their fathers beat their mothers were also more violently abusive towards their own children.

According to Rathbone-McCuan (1980), 1 of 2 children mistreated violently by their parents attacks the parents later on, compared with 1 in 400 children reared non-violently. On the other hand, Pillemer (1986) did not find an association between being physically punished as a child and becoming an elder abuser later. "While the data reported here are limited, they do not generally support the hypothesis that children who abuse elderly parents were themselves victims of abuse" (Pillemer 1986, 250). It appears, then, that further research is needed to test this particular hypothesis of transgenerational family violence as a plausible contributing factor to elder abuse and neglect. A key issue to be investigated is whether intergenerational transmission of violence occurs through a modelling process in which children observe their parents abusing grandparents or whether it originates from a subculture of violence in which family members are violent in general.

Web of Dependencies

It has been stated in the literature that the most likely victims of elder abuse are older women with severe physical and/or mental impairments

(Block and Sinnott 1979; Lau and Kosberg 1979; O'Malley et al. 1979; Wolf et al. 1982; Gioglio and Blakemore 1983; Giordano and Giordano 1984; Hall and Andrew 1984). The belief that dependency is a major cause of elder abuse is probably the most widely held explanation of elder abuse and neglect (Pillemer 1986).

> Dependency is typically defined as requiring assistance from another person or persons to continue living in the community. Help can be provided in such areas as the basic activities of daily living (dressing, bathing, cooking, shopping, etc.); financial support; or emotional support and companionship. [Pillemer 1985a, 147]

It is hypothesized that, because of physical or mental impairments, the elderly person becomes increasingly dependent upon his or her caregiver for emotional, physical, and financial support. This may lead to resentment and severe stress on the part of the caregiver. As a result of this dependence, the elderly person becomes especially vulnerable to abuse (Douglass et al. 1980). In addition, it is suggested that learned helplessness contributes further to already potentially abusive relationships, since elders may increasingly feel that they have lost control over their lives and cannot do anything to remedy the situation (Giordano and Giordano 1984). Pillemer (1986), Pillemer and Finkelhor (1989), and Bristowe and Collins (1989) found, however, that abused elders were neither more physically impaired nor in poorer health than non-abused elders. Furthermore, in certain respects the abused elders were significantly less impaired than the non-abused elders.

It has also been suggested that it may, in fact, be the abuser who is dependent on the victim. According to Pillemer, "dependency seems to play a critical role in elder abuse, but it is not yet clear who is depending on whom in these abusive relationships" (1986, 244). For example, in some situations the caregivers themselves may be functionally impaired (Hudson and Johnson 1986). In addition, it has been reported that, in many cases, abusive caretakers are dependent on their victims for financial support and/or housing. For example, Wolf et al. (1982) found that in two-thirds of the cases the perpetrator was financially dependent on the victim. Pillemer's results (1985a) indicated that 64 percent of abusers were financially dependent on their victims and 55 percent were dependent on their victims for housing. In contrast to non-abusive caregivers, the abusive caregivers were found to have significantly more dependencies on the elderly in four areas: (1) housing; (2) household repair; (3) financial assistance; and (4) transportation.

However, not all dependent relationships among elders and caregivers result in elder abuse and neglect. It is suggested that additional factors are involved in those situations that lead to abuse. For example, a triggering event or crisis of some kind may precipitate abuse (Quinn and

Tomita 1986). On the basis of these findings, it is apparent that further research is needed to test the relationship between dependencies and elder abuse and neglect.

Personality Traits of the Abuser

The personality traits of the abuser are also believed to be important factors that may contribute to abusive behavior. The personality traits of the abuser have been referred to as the intra-individual dynamics or psychopathology of the abuser or caregiver. There is much controversy surrounding the hypothesis that the personality traits of the abuser contribute to abuse because it is often considered too simplistic and because the literature cannot determine or agree upon what pathological traits are characteristic of abusers. Research in this area has neither confirmed nor refuted the hypothesis (Giordano and Giordano 1984; Pillemer 1986).

Lau and Kosberg (1979) describe the abusive caregiver as a "non-normal" adult child who is mentally ill, retarded, or alcoholic. In most cases, these adult children have been previously cared for all their life. Douglass et al. (1980) refer to the "flawed development" of the abusive caregiver that has resulted from problems that originated in early childhood. Wolf et al. (1984) found that 31 percent of abusers had histories of psychiatric illnesses and 43 percent had substance abuse problems. In his comparison of abused and non-abused elders, Pillemer (1986) found that abused elders (79 percent) were more likely to report that their abusive caregiver had psychological or emotional problems than were non-abused elders (24 percent). In addition, it was reported that abusers (45.2 percent) were more likely than non-abusive caregivers (7.1 percent) to be alcoholic.

The relationship between alcohol abuse and family violence has gained strong support as a causal factor of elder abuse (Lau and Kosberg 1979; O'Malley et al. 1979; Giordano and Giordano 1984). For example, in terms of Canadian research (Shell 1982; Bristowe and Collins 1989), it has been reported that alcoholism is the most frequently identified high-risk factor characteristic of abusive caregivers. Bristowe and Collins (1989) found that the most obvious differences between abusive and non-abusive caregivers included the much greater use of alcohol among abusive caregivers, in addition to the greater likelihood of caregiver confusion. For example, 88 percent of the abusive caregivers reported alcohol use, compared with 30 percent of the non-abusive caregivers. In addition, Bristowe and Collins found that greater alcohol consumption was associated with more severe and more frequent abuse.

Filial Crisis

The failure of adult children to resolve the filial crisis has been proposed by several theorists as a viable factor that contributes to elder abuse and neglect (Block and Sinnott 1979; Lau and Kosberg 1979; Giordano and Giordano 1984). In such cases, parent-child conflicts that began in adolescence continue into later life. When the adult child attempts to use old defensive techniques, the original problems in the parent-child relationship escalate. As a result, the child may abuse his or her elderly parent. This factor has received little attention in the literature, and empirical findings have not been presented.

Internal and External Stressors

The responsibility of caring for a dependent, elderly parent or relative can be overwhelming. Abusers often lack understanding and knowledge of the aging process and hold unrealistic expectations of the capabilities of the elderly person (Chen et al. 1981). In many cases, the elderly person is perceived to be a source of stress by the abuser (Pennsylvania Department of Aging 1982; Quinn and Tomita 1986). For example, O'Malley et al. (1979) reported that, in 69 percent of the abuse occurrences, the abuser found the victim to be a great source of stress because of the high levels of physical and emotional care required. The caregiver, as well as the entire family, may find caring for an elderly person to be a very stressful situation and this may result in abuse of the elderly person (Block and Sinnott 1979; O'Malley et al. 1979; Douglass et al. 1980; Rathbone-McCuan 1980; Pedrick-Cornell and Gelles 1982; Shell 1982; Giordano and Giordano 1984).

When caregivers spend many long hours providing physical and emotional care to a frail elderly relative, they may become exhausted and anxious (Giordano and Giordano 1984). Adults who assume responsibility for their elderly parents, as well as their own children, can feel that their efforts are not sufficiently recognized in exchange for the care they are providing. They may feel resentful, angry, and frustrated, and feel the needs of their family are being subordinated to those of the elderly person (Pedrick-Cornell and Gelles 1982). Situtions such as these may become abusive.

Several studies found that it was not unusual for a 65- to 70-year-old son or daughter to be attempting to care for an 85- to 90-year old parent (Walker 1983; Steinmetz 1988). In many cases, 65-year-old caregivers have difficulty caring for their own needs and therefore are frustrated as a result of the additional burden and responsibility of an elderly parent. This frustration frequently results in physical acting out against the elderly person.

In addition, external stressors have been widely recognized as major factors that are related to family violence (Giordano and Giordano 1984). External stressors have also been found to play an important role in relation to elder abuse and neglect (Block and Sinnott 1979; Lau and Kosberg 1979; Douglass et al. 1980; Pennsylvania Department of Aging 1982; Shell

1982; Giordano and Giordano 1984; Hudson and Johnson 1986; Pillemer 1986). According to Hudson and Johnson's (1986) review of the literature, it has been consistently found that both the abused elder and the abusive caregiver experience excessive amounts of stress.

The effects of socio-cultural variables such as overcrowding, unemployment, alcohol and drug abuse, and financial problems have been examined in the literature. O'Malley et al. (1979) found that 75 percent of abusers experienced some form of stress. Giordano and Giordano (1984) reported that studies have found that abusers are likely to be alcoholics who have experienced considerable external stress, such as a job loss or a long-term medical problem. Although stress appears to intensify the potential for abuse, it is not a reliable predictor, since most families experience stress at one time or another and do not abuse their elderly members (Hudson and Johnson 1986; Pillemer 1986). Therefore, it is important to examine how abusive situations differ from non-abusive ones in terms of the household's experiences with stress and the coping skills used in response to stress.

Social Isolation

Families characterized by violence are often found to be socially isolated, since violence tends to be hidden when it is recognized as illegitimate (Gelles 1979). It is suggested that it is less likely for family violence to erupt when friends or relatives live nearby and interact frequently. The presence of an active support group may deter highly illegitimate behavior, such as elder abuse. In addition, social support resources may act as moderators of stress and facilitate coping with crises, as well as reduce feelings of burden on the part of caregivers of the elderly (Pillemer 1986; Wolf 1986).

Pillemer (1986) found that abused elders were more likely to have fewer contacts with friends and family members than non-abused elders. In addition, abused elders were significantly more likely to be unsatisfied with their social relationships. Pillemer goes on to suggest, however, that these results do not prove that social isolation causes elder abuse. Rather, he proposes, elder abuse causes social isolation.

Ageism: Negative Attitudes towards the Elderly

According to Giordano and Giordano (1984, 235), "patterns of elder abuse and neglect may be reinforced by negative stereotypes toward elderly people and their roles in society." It is hypothesized that misconceptions or negative attitudes towards the elderly may contribute significantly to the creation of situations conducive to abuse. These negative attitudes dehumanize elderly persons and thus make it easier for them to be victimized, while the abuser feels no guilt or remorse.

Quinn and Tomita (1986) refer to ageism as a pervasive prejudice against elders that involves systematic discrimination and stereotyping against people because they are old. Old age is viewed as a disability that is synonymous with a loss of personal powers and control over one's life. Block and Sinnott (1979) note that attitudes, misconceptions, and distortions about aging and the aged call for more research into the role of ageism in situations of elder abuse and neglect. Furthermore, they suggest that the elderly themselves may view abusive treatment as deserved, unavoidable, or inconsequential, since they too may internalize society's negative attitudes and stereotypes.

For example, even among practitioners who work with the elderly, Douglass et al. (1980) found that 20 percent believed the victims were in some way partially responsible for their own neglect or abuse. The respondents suggested that some elderly have difficult personalities or personal habits, or levels of dependency that contribute to their own abuse or neglect. In addition, Shell (1982) found that most Manitoban practitioners she interviewed considered physical, psychological, and financial abuse to be unintentional on the part of the caregiver.

Institutional Factors

Several authors have suggested factors that may contribute to the abuse and neglect of elderly residents in institutional settings in the United States (Townsend 1971; Hahn 1976; Moss and Halamandaris 1977; Mercer 1983; Vladeck 1980; Pillemer 1988). These factors include: (1) the lack of comprehensive and consistent policy with respect to the infirm elderly; (2) the fact that the long-term care system is characterized by inherent or built-in financial incentives that contribute towards poor care; (3) the powerlessness and vulnerability of elderly residents; (4) the lack of enforcement of nursing home standards; and (5) the lack of highly qualified and trained staff. Each of these is discussed briefly below.

Gains have been made with respect to the long-term care of the elderly, primarily through the enactment of medical programs in the United States. However, the benefits provided remain woefully short of what is needed. For example, over one-fifth of elderly adults require some degree of protective services, ranging from personal care (e.g., assistance in dressing, bathing, eating) to intensive nursing care. According to Moss and Halamandaris (1977), of the 4.5 million older Americans who need such help, only 1.5 million receive it. Most of this assistance is found in nursing homes, and nursing home care may be inappropriate.

Most available data suggest that Canada institutionalizes a substantial proportion of its elderly, about 7.5 percent (Forbes et al. 1987), implying that inappropriate placements occur. As well, the provision of institutional long-term care for the elderly varies remarkably between the different provinces, and there is split responsibility for the elderly among different government departments for service (see Forbes et al. 1987 for a full discussion of these problems). Whether or not these conditions would create the potential for abuse has not been explored in Canada.

Enormous amounts of money flow through nursing homes, and the industry as a whole is highly profitable, particularly in the United States (Stathopoulous 1983). In Canada, the proportion of nursing homes run for profit varies from province to province (29 percent of nursing home beds in Manitoba compared to 37 percent in British Columbia), and provincially insured nursing home benefits are unequally applied across provinces. Whether the profit motive and the various systems of payment would contribute to elder abuse is a question yet to be answered. For example, Forbes et al. (1987) suggest that a proprietary nursing home may, for financial reasons, refuse to admit someone who requires considerable care but does not reach the criteria for a chronic care hospital. This patient could then be placed in a care facility offering a lower level of care, where staff are not equipped to deal with the patient's care demands, and the chances for abuse or neglect could perhaps increase.

Vladeck (1980) suggests that the opportunity for crime in the nursing home industry is vast and that this is partly due to the weaknesses and vulnerability of the residents. In many cases, especially cases involving material abuse, elderly residents are often unaware of the fraudulent practices taking place. In other cases, residents refrain from reporting incidents out of fear of reprisals from their abusive caregivers.

The fact that so many nursing home facilities are substandard and so few homes are penalized or closed strongly suggests that there are shortcomings in the enforcement of nursing home standards in the United States. Although standards may be identified, they are not effective unless they are faithfully enforced. Current practices, such as infrequent inspections, advance notice of inspections, the treatment of inspections as bureaucratic rituals, relationships between the regulator and the regulated, the disregard of inspectors' recommendations, and the use of political influence to keep some homes open, contribute to the lack of enforcement of nursing home standards. Furthermore, the chances of being caught are low and the odds of being punished in some proportion to the size of the crime are almost infinitesimal (Vladeck 1980).

In Canada, Kane and Kane (1985) have noted that the system of inspection in Ontario nursing homes, like that in the United States, is flawed because prior notification allows the home to prepare in advance for an inspection. At the same time, the results of inspections are not public information, so it is difficult to know if abuse occurs in these nursing homes. The system of accreditation in Ontario is voluntary, operated by the Canadian Council on Hospital Accreditation, which has been seen to be self-serving. There is obviously some problem with this system, because a consumer advocate group was formed in Ontario to counteract the lobbying efforts made by the providers of long-term care. The reports of this consumer group, Concerned Friends of Ontario Citizens in Care Facilities, would suggest that some elder neglect if not abuse exists.

It has been reported that 80 percent to 90 percent of formal caregiving services are provided by untrained and unlicensed aids and orderlies (Townsend 1971; Moss and Halamandaris 1977; Vladeck 1980; Stathopoulos 1983; J.E. Hudson 1986; Jorgensen 1986) in the United States. Furthermore, physicians are usually absent from nursing homes and there are few qualified nurses.

This situation is, perhaps, not as serious in Canada, but the truth of the matter is that we have little information about adequate levels of education, in-service training, or staffing patterns for Canadian nursing homes other than what is contained in the various sets of standards for staffing and services in institutions (see Forbes et al. 1987).

In a recent article, Pillemer (1988) provides a critical review of the literature regarding elderly patients in nursing homes. In addition, on the basis of his review of the research findings, he proposes a theoretical model of potential causes of elder abuse in institutions to guide future research. This is an admirable step forward in this field, since little theoretical work has been conducted in the area of elder abuse, especially in regard to elder abuse that occurs in institutional settings.

Pillemer's (1988) model includes exogenous variables, such as supply of nursing home beds and unemployment rate, as well as nursing home environment variables, such as custodial orientation, level of care, size, rates, cost of patient care, ownership status, staff-patient ratio, and staff turnover rate. In addition, staff characteristics, including education, age, gender, position, experience, and burnout are examined. Lastly, Pillemer suggests that the health of patients, their degree of social isolation, and gender are also important factors in this model. The model considers patient maltreatment to include physical violence, verbal aggression, and neglect.

In a test of part of his theory, Pillemer and Moore (1989) found evidence that situational variables that directly affect the quality of staff-patient interactions appear to predict physical and psychological abuse. Staff who reported that they frequently thought about quitting, who viewed patients as childlike, and who had high rates of burnout and frequent conflicts with patients were more likely to commit abuse.

Thus, a variety of factors have been reported to be related to low-quality nursing home care that may result in physical, psychological, or material injury to the elderly resident. However, efforts have been made to correct many of these deficiencies, primarily through legislation stipulating nursing home requirements and standards. Further research is needed, however, to examine the impact of current nursing home conditions on the likelihood of abuse and neglect of the elderly residents.

CONCLUSIONS

Theories of elder abuse and neglect are primarily based on general theories developed and applied in the field of family violence. Three distinct theories were identified: (1) the situational model, which emphasizes internal and external stressors such as life crises; (2) the social exchange model, which stresses the importance of networks of dependencies; and (3) the symbolic interaction model, which emphasizes the role of modelling violence. Theories of domestic violence, by definition, have focused on abuse by informal caregivers as opposed to formal caregivers. Theories explaining elder abuse and neglect by formal caregivers are only now being considered. At the same time, there has been little application of the theories found in the field of social gerontology that may have some potential for explaining elder abuse and neglect.

In addition to the theories referred to above, specific variables have been associated with elder abuse. These variables include: (1) transgenerational family violence; (2) web of dependencies; (3) personality traits of the abuser; (4) filial crisis; (5) internal and external stressors; (6) social isolation; (7) societal attitudes towards the elderly; and (8) institutional factors.

In short, it would appear that a limited number of perspectives, which have sometimes been viewed as competing explanations, have been proffered to explain elder abuse and neglect (Phillips 1986, 197). There also appears to be a classificatory catch-all of causal factors associated with elder abuse and neglect. All of this would suggest that no single theoretical approach is likely to account for the separate events subsumed under elder abuse and neglect; that the scope of theory generation must be broadened beyond the family violence and caregiver stress hypotheses; and that hypotheses must be subjected to the rigors of empirical testing.

CHAPTER 3

GENERAL LEGAL SAFEGUARDS FOR VULNERABLE ADULTS IN CANADA

As is discussed in Chapter 1, several Canadian provinces and most jurisdictions in the United States have responded to the problem of elder abuse by enacting special adult protection legislation, usually including a mandatory reporting requirement. Before examining this type of legislation, it is important to consider the extent to which other existing laws afford protection to vulnerable adults in Canada. One should not necessarily assume that the problem of elder abuse can be addressed only by means of special protection legislation. As Gordon et al. point out:

> [I]n a rush to state what the law does *not* accomplish, there has been a failure to explore carefully the full range of existing options. In the context of abuse and neglect in the family setting, several avenues might be pursued. [Gordon et al. 1986, 60–61]

PHYSICAL AND EMOTIONAL ABUSE

The *Criminal Code*, R.S.C. 1985, c. C–46, contains a number of provisions that (at least in theory) afford vulnerable adults protection from physical abuse by punishing the perpetrator. For example, charges can be laid in relation to assault (s. 265), assault causing bodily harm (s. 267), aggravated assault (s. 268), unlawfully causing bodily harm (s. 269), sexual assault (s. 271), and aggravated sexual assault (s. 273). With respect to emotional abuse, the *Criminal Code* creates a number of offences that have potential application — offences that the Law Reform Commission of Canada (1987, 64) describes as "crimes against psychological integrity" — such as intimidation (s. 423) and assault by means of threats (s. 265).

From a practical point of view, however, the criminal law is ineffective in protecting the victims of elder abuse. This is true of domestic violence in general. All too often, "practice falls sadly short of theory" (Law Reform Commission of Canada 1984, 37). Victims of elder abuse are often unable or unwilling to complain to the police (Sengstock and Hwalek 1986; Rozovsky and Rozovsky 1987; Sharpe 1988). It is difficult in many cases to obtain the necessary evidence to prove the offence beyond a reasonable doubt, and thus the authorities may be unwilling to proceed with a prosecution (Sharpe 1988). Even if a criminal prosecution is brought, this will normally be of little assistance to the victim; prosecution focuses on punishing the offender rather than on helping the victim (Metcalf 1986; Sharpe 1988).

Not only may reliance on the criminal law be ineffective, it may make the situation worse. As Metcalf (1986) notes, the victim may face retaliation from the abuser following a complaint to the police. Metcalf also points out that the abuser may be the victim's only means of support; if the abuser is imprisoned, the victim may have to be placed in institutional care.

Recent government directives in many parts of Canada have led to a significant change in police practice in cases of spouse abuse. The police have been directed to lay charges and to arrest, when appropriate, rather than placing the onus on the victim to press charges (Endicott 1987). This may have an impact in cases of elder/spouse abuse. Also, some police forces have been active in developing directives and protocols for responding to elder abuse. For example, the Metro Toronto police force appointed a full-time liaison officer in July 1988 to deal exclusively with the problem of elder abuse, including policy development (Advocacy Centre for the Elderly 1988).

NEGLECT

Section 215 of the *Criminal Code*, R.S.C. 1985, s. C–46, imposes a duty to provide necessaries of life to a person under one's charge if that person is unable, because of age, illness, or other cause, to withdraw from that charge and provide himself or herself with the necessities of life. Failure to perform this duty, without lawful excuse, is a criminal offence if it endangers life or causes (or is likely to cause) permanent injury to health (Gordon et al. 1986; Robertson 1987). The most common offence prosecuted under this section is the failure to provide necessary medical aid to a person under one's charge.

In the context of neglect, provincial legislation is wider in scope, since it gives the elderly person a legally enforceable right to support rather than merely imposing a criminal sanction on the offender. Every Canadian province has legislation that requires children over the age of majority to provide reasonable support for their parents if the parents are unable to maintain themselves. In most provinces, this obligation arises only if the parents' inability to support themselves is due to factors such as destitution, age, infirmity, or illness. However, in some provinces the duty goes beyond this (Gordon et al. 1986; Robertson 1987; Steel 1988). In Ontario, for example, the *Family Law Act 1986*, S.O. 1986, c. 4, s. 32, imposes a duty on children to support parents in accordance with their need, to the extent that the child is able to do so. In addition, a legal duty of mutual support is imposed on spouses (Davies 1984).

Of particular importance in the context of neglect is the power to enter premises in cases of perceived emergency (Blake 1983). As a general rule, a person who enters another's premises without consent commits trespass. Even in the case of police officers, there is no general power of entry except in the course of effecting a lawful arrest or acting under a search warrant pursuant to the *Criminal Code*. There is, however, a possible common law defence of necessity if the entrant's actions are reasonably necessary for the protection of property or life (Law Reform Commission of Canada 1987). For example, in *Re Children's Aid Society of Western Manitoba and Daniels* (1981), 128 D.L.R. (3d) 751, the Manitoba Court of Appeal held that police officers were legally entitled to enter premises without consent when they reasonably believed that the life of an occupant was in danger. Despite this principle, the power of entry in situations of emergency remains, at best, unclear.

In addition to the common law defence of necessity, public health legislation in most provinces contains powers of intervention that could possibly be used when a person's living conditions constitute a public health hazard (Gordon et al. 1986). However, as Sharpe (1987) notes, these provisions are ill suited to most situations of elder abuse, and offer little in the way of assistance to an endangered person living in an environment of abuse or neglect. The legislation could, of course, be amended to provide for a power of entry in cases of perceived emergency. For example, the equivalent legislation in British Columbia enables a medical officer of health to intervene in situations where an aged or incapacitated person is living in unsanitary or dangerous conditions and is unable to care for himself or herself (Gordon et al. 1986). The Ontario Advisory Committee on Substitute Decision Making for Mentally Incapable Persons (1987) recommended that the Ontario legislation be amended to include such a provision.

FINANCIAL ABUSE AND EXPLOITATION

Most instances of financial abuse and exploitation of the elderly constitute offences under Parts IX and X of the *Criminal Code*, R.S.C. 1985, c. C–46, such as theft, misuse of a power of attorney, breach of trust, forgery, fraud, and extortion. The potential criminal sanction can be severe; for example, the maximum penalty for forgery is 14 years' imprisonment (s. 367). In addition, the offender can be ordered, pursuant to section 725 of the *Code*, to pay compensation to the victim and to restore any property obtained by the crime.

Some protection from financial abuse and exploitation is also afforded by the common law concepts of fraud, duress, undue influence, and unconscionability (Waddams 1984; Fridman 1986). If a person has entered into a transaction (for example, the sale of a house) as a result of another's threats, improper pressure, or other unconscionable conduct, the law will intervene to set aside the agreement or grant some alternative form of relief. There is also special legislation in most provinces dealing with unconscionable transactions.

The protection offered by these laws is limited by the fact that they are reactive in nature. They either punish the wrongdoer or compensate the victim, but (other than having a possible deterrent effect) they do not prevent or detect financial abuse, nor are they intended to do so.

The law can, however, perform a preventative function in this area by regulating specific situations in which the elderly are especially vulnerable to financial abuse. One such situation involves powers of attorney, particularly enduring powers of attorney. In common law, a power of attorney is revoked if the grantor becomes mentally incapacitated. Most provinces have recognized the inadequacy of this common law rule, and have enacted legislation that provides for a power of attorney to continue notwithstanding the subsequent incapacity of the grantor (Gordon et al. 1986; Robertson 1987; Alberta Law Reform Institute 1990). This has considerable advantages, not the least of which is that it enables individuals to arrange for the management of their affairs in the event of their incapacity, thereby avoiding the necessity of proceedings under the mental incompetency legislation for the appointment of a committee of the person's estate.

Despite its undeniable advantages, the enduring power of attorney, by its very nature, is susceptible to abuse and exploitation. A number of writers have questioned whether present safeguards are adequate (Harewood 1981; Shell 1982; Kapp 1983; Gordon et al. 1986). Particular concern has been expressed with the fact that a person who is granted a power of attorney by an elderly person is not required to report to the grantor or to anyone else, and thus it is possible that finances may be misused without the elderly person's knowledge. Moreover, Gordon et al. (1986) note that:

> [I]t is apparent that many durable powers are being donated by individuals at a time when they are unaware of the implications of their actions, possibly subject to undue influence, and are probably open to financial abuse. The Ontario Public Trustee contends that many powers are signed only a few days before the donor is certified as incompetent by a psychiatrist and that there are a suspiciously high number of such cases. Short of launching costly legal proceedings, there is no procedure that the Trustee can follow in order to rescind a power which is donated under dubious circumstances. [R.M. Gordon, S.N. Verdun-Jones, and D.J. MacDougall, *Standing in Their Shoes: Guardianship, Trusteeship and The Elderly Canadian* (Burnaby, B.C.: Simon Fraser University, Criminology Research Centre, 1986), 331. Reproduced with permission.]

In Ontario, the *Powers of Attorney Act*, R.S.O. 1980, c. 386, ss. 6, 9, 10, contains a number of safeguards against misuse of an enduring power of attorney. The Act provides that the power of attorney must be executed in the presence of a witness, and that the attorney and his or her spouse are ineligible to act as witnesses. Once the donor has become incapacitated, any interested person (including the Public Trustee) can apply to the court for an order directing the attorney to pass accounts. The court is also empowered to remove and replace an attorney on the application of the Public Trustee or any interested person. These provisions were recommended by the Ontario Law Reform Commission (1972) and were viewed by the Commission as essential precautions against improper conduct on the part of the attorney. The Fram Committee recently recommended that the safeguards be strengthened by (among other things) increasing the minimum number of witnesses to two and requiring each witness to certify in writing that the donor was mentally capable of managing property when the power of attorney was signed (Ontario Advisory Committee on Substitute Decision Making for Mentally Incapable Persons 1987).

Additional precautions are certainly possible, and perhaps necessary. For example, in British Columbia the *Community Care Facility Act*, R.S.B.C. 1979, c. 57, s. 12(2)(g), provides that the operator of a nursing home or other facility cannot be appointed under a power of attorney granted by a resident of the facility (Gordon et al. 1986; Robertson 1987).

Another safeguard involves registration. Both the Ontario Law Reform Commission (1972) and the Manitoba Law Reform Commission (1974) were in favor of introducing a requirement that enduring powers of attorney be registered with the surrogate or county court. In neither case was this recommendation implemented by the legislature. However, recent legislation in England has adopted a registration requirement (Puttick 1985; Wilkinson 1986; Alberta Law Reform Institute 1990). Gordon et al. (1986) describe registration as the ''only viable solution'' to the misuse of powers of attorney, and they recommend a requirement that *all* powers of attorney (other than those intended to be in effect for less than four weeks) be registered with the Public Trustee.

The problem with additional precautions in this area is that they may conflict with, and even frustrate, the basic purpose of the enduring power of attorney. Its aim is to provide individuals with a relatively simple method of arranging in advance for the management of their financial affairs after they become incapacitated. The more the law introduces formalities and requirements, the less attractive this option becomes for the donor. As a number of other Law Reform Commissions have noted in recommending against a registration requirement, the statutory scheme should be kept as simple as possible (Law Reform Commission of British Columbia 1975; Australian Law Reform Commission 1987; Newfoundland Law Reform Commission 1988; Alberta Law Reform Institute 1990).

The power of attorney has traditionally been used for purposes of financial management. However, in recent years support has grown in the

United States for applying the power-of-attorney model to medical decision making. This would enable individuals to designate someone to consent (or withhold consent) to medical treatment on their behalf in the event of their becoming mentally incapacitated (Kapp 1983). In May 1988, the government of Nova Scotia brought in a *Medical Consent Act*, S.N.S. 1988, c. 14, which adopts this model. The use of the power-of-attorney model in areas of personal care, including health care, was also recommended by the Ontario Advisory Committee on Substitute Decision Making for Mentally Incapable Persons (1987).

ELDER ABUSE IN AN INSTITUTION

For several years, consumer and advocacy groups have been calling for tighter control and regulation of nursing homes and similar facilities (Gordon et al. 1986). In Ontario, the Coalition for Nursing Home Reform has been particularly active. The importance of a patient advocate system has also been emphasized (Regan 1977; Douglas et al. 1985; Ontario Advisory Committee on Substitute Decision Making for Mentally Incapable Persons 1987; Ontario Ministry of the Attorney General 1987). These calls for reform are, in part, a response to the growing evidence of abuse and neglect of the elderly in institutions. There are strong indications of a link between elder abuse and the widespread privatization policy in nursing home care (Gordon and Verdun-Jones 1985; Gordon et al. 1986). Moreover, as the Ontario Ministry of the Attorney General notes, "[i]nstitutionalization, of its very nature, creates vulnerability" (1987, 56).

The Ontario government has recently responded to these concerns by introducing amendments to the *Nursing Homes Act*, R.S.O. 1980, c. 320. The *Act to Amend the Nursing Homes Act*, S.O. 1987, c. 20, made a number of important changes to the regulation of these facilities. Two aspects of the 1987 Act stand out as particularly significant. First, the legislation introduces a mandatory reporting requirement in cases of abuse, neglect, or improper treatment of residents in nursing homes. Section 17a(1) provides that:

> A person other than a resident who has reasonable grounds to suspect that a resident has suffered or may suffer harm as a result of unlawful conduct, improper or incompetent treatment or care or neglect shall forthwith report the suspicion and the information upon which it is based to the Director.

Section 17a(5) provides that health care professionals must comply with this duty, notwithstanding the confidentiality of the information on which the report is based. On the receipt of a report, the Director is required to investigate the matter immediately.

In April 1988, the Ontario Police Commission issued a directive requesting that police officers develop educational programs on elder abuse for residents and staff in long-term care institutions, and that officers conduct a thorough investigation of any alleged abuse in nursing homes and other long-term care institutions (Advocacy Centre for the Elderly 1988).

The other significant aspect of the recent amendments to the Ontario *Nursing Homes Act* is the enactment of a Residents' Bill of Rights, a concept common in several jurisdictions in the United States (Phillips 1980; Caldwell and Kapp 1981; Opperman 1981). Section 1a(2) lists 19 "rights" of residents that licensees of nursing homes must ensure are fully respected and promoted. These include the following statements:

1. Every resident has the right to be treated with courtesy and respect and in a way that fully recognizes the resident's dignity and individuality and to be free from mental and physical abuse.
2. Every resident has the right to be properly sheltered, fed, clothed, groomed and cared for in a manner consistent with his or her needs. . . .
18. Every resident has the right to live in a safe and clean environment.

The list also contains a number of references to the right of residents to personal privacy. The importance of this aspect of institutional life cannot be overemphasized. Bissett-Johnson (1986) refers to the invasion of personal privacy in institutions as a form of abuse — "clean abuse" (Bissett-Johnson 1986, 272).

The concept of a resident's bill of rights has not escaped criticism. It has been suggested that it serves no meaningful purpose, since many of the "rights" are vague and unenforceable (such as the right to be treated with courtesy and respect), and also that it is misleading in implying that the rights of residents are limited to those mentioned in the statutory list (Rozovsky 1980; Rozovsky and Rozovsky 1987).

Government regulation is not the only legal response to elder abuse in institutions. Tort law may also play a role in safeguarding the interests of residents by imposing liability on the facility for harm suffered by a resident (Johnson 1985; Gordon et al. 1986). For example, in a recent Saskatchewan case, a nursing home was held liable in damages for an assault by one resident on another (Robertson 1987, 389). In the United States, the number of lawsuits against nursing home owners involving abuse and neglect of the elderly has risen sharply in recent years (Nemore 1985).

GUARDIANSHIP AND TRUSTEESHIP

There is little doubt that, with the exceptions of Alberta, Saskatchewan, and Quebec, Canadian guardianship legislation is in need of fundamental reform. Gordon et al. (1986) describe Canadian guardianship legislation as "an anachronism"; Sharpe (1987) describes it as "antiquated." Robertson (1987) states that, measured by the standards that guardianship law ought to achieve, Canadian law "fails miserably" and is in need of radical reform. Even the Supreme Court of Canada — in *Re Eve* (1986),

31 D.L.R. (4th) 1 at 16 — has said that the present Canadian law of guardianship is "pitifully unclear with repect of some basic issues." With the exceptions of Alberta, Saskatchewan, and Quebec, Canadian guardianship legislation fails to provide adequate criteria for the appointment of a guardian and fails to specify the powers and duties of a guardian. The Law Reform Commission of Saskatchewan (1981), commenting on that province's previous guardianship legislation (which in this respect was typical of most Canadian provinces), stated that its "procedures . . . are cumbersome, its provisions inadequate, and its language archaic" (Law Reform Commission of Saskatchewan 1981, 3).

Most important of all, Canadian guardianship laws adopt an inflexible "all or nothing approach" and fail to provide for the appointment of a guardian with limited powers. Once a guardian is appointed on behalf of a person, the latter loses complete control over decision making affecting his or her life (Law Reform Commission of Saskatchewan 1983; Gordon et al. 1986; Robertson 1987; Hughes 1988). The only exceptions are Alberta's *Dependent Adults Act*, R.S.A. 1980, c. D–32, Saskatchewan's *Dependent Adults Act*, S.S. 1989-90, c. D–25.1, and the equivalent provisions of the *Civil Code* of Quebec, which are based on the philosophy of the least restrictive alternative. The Alberta Act authorizes the court to grant the guardian only those powers necessary to assist the dependent adult in making reasonable decisions regarding his or her person (Christie 1982, 1984; Gordon et al. 1986; Robertson 1987; Hughes 1988). Similar provisions were introduced in Quebec as a result of amendments to the *Civil Code* in 1989, which were proclaimed in force on April 15, 1990 — Statutes of Quebec, c. 54. The Saskatchewan legislation, which was passed in 1989 and proclaimed in force on March 1, 1990, is very similar to the Alberta model.

Another important aspect of the Alberta legislation is the creation of the office of Public Guardian. The Public Guardian discharges a number of different functions, one of which is to act as a form of safety net for those in need of guardianship. If no one is willing to bring an application for the appointment of a guardian for someone who is in need of guardianship, the Public Guardian must do so. Likewise, the Public Guardian will be appointed if there is no other suitable person to act as guardian (Christie 1982, 1984; Robertson 1987).

It is clear that present guardianship laws, because of their many deficiencies, are ineffective as a means of addressing the problem of elder abuse. As Sadavoy (1983) and McLaughlin (1979) point out, the legislation is not flexible enough to allow rapid intervention in emergency cases. However, in many jurisdictions, including Ontario, Manitoba, Newfoundland, and Yukon, the legislation is currently under review (Gordon et al. 1987) and reform seems inevitable. This raises the question of what role future guardianship legislation should play in responding to the problem of elder abuse.

McLaughlin recommends that "guardianship law *not* be used as the basis of any attempt to deal with the issues of neglect, abuse or exploitation of at-risk adults" (1979, 91), although he tentatively favours the concept of temporary guardianship for crisis situations, as does Borovoy (1982). However, McLaughlin goes on to note that, although guardianship may be ineffective as a means of crisis *intervention*, it can be important for crisis *prevention* if it is in place in advance. Where a guardian has been appointed, and is properly discharging his or her duty to protect and enhance the best interests of the adult person, the potential for neglect and abuse is likely to be reduced significantly.

The appropriate relationship between adult protection legislation and guardianship is a difficult issue, particularly in view of the different objectives underlying the two concepts. Adult protection legislation is directed primarily at emergency intervention and the provision of services, whereas the main purpose of guardianship is to provide for long-term care and assistance and substitute decision making (Gordon et al. 1986; Hughes 1988). Metcalf (1986) criticizes the use of guardianship in cases where limited intervention would alleviate the problem, and she emphasizes that this is contrary to the principle of the least restrictive alternative. On the other hand, Gordon et al. (1986) point out that the guardianship model could be adapted to include the provision of temporary guardianship as a means of crisis intervention. For example, the *Civil Code* of Quebec was recently amended to provide that a court may appoint a guardian where this is required to save the person from grave harm. Gordon et al. (1986) recommend that:

> Rather than having these problems addressed in separate legislation, it is desirable that they form part of a "guardianship package." After all, long-term guardianship may be a core strategy in planning the management of a particular case. A guardianship statute should, therefore, make provision for the reporting of, and response to, abuse and neglect; that is, both the immediate protection of an endangered adult and the provision of a temporary guardian for a short period of time. If the case management plan included long-term guardianship, then the temporary guardian should be required to make an appropriate application to a court. [R.M. Gordon, S.N. Verdun-Jones, and D.J. MacDougall, *Standing in Their Shoes: Guardianship, Trusteeship and The Elderly Canadian* (Burnaby, B.C.: Simon Fraser University, Criminology Research Centre, 1986), 589–90. Reproduced with permission.]

This recommendation has considerable merit, but it may also have one very real disadvantage. The integration of adult protection intervention into an omnibus "guardianship package" may imply that guardianship should be the primary, if not the only, response to elder abuse. This would be unfortunate. In many cases of elder abuse, guardianship — even for a temporary period — is inappropriate, and a less intrusive alternative is needed. As numerous writers, including Gordon et al. (1986), have emphasized, it is essential, when considering the appropriate response to elder abuse, to keep in mind the principle of the least restrictive alternative (Horstman 1975; Harewood 1981; Note 1983; Sharpe 1983, 1988; Sloan 1983; Metcalf 1986; Hughes 1988).

CONCLUSIONS

This chapter examined the extent to which existing laws in Canada other than special adult protection legislation are relevant to the protection of vulnerable adults in general and, more specifically, of the elderly.

There are a number of provisions in the *Criminal Code* that could afford vulnerable adults some protection from physical and emotional abuse. For example, charges can be laid against perpetrators for physical assault and assault by means of threats. However, it is generally assumed that criminal law is ineffective in dealing with domestic abuse situations, including elder abuse. This assumption is based on the following circumstances: (1) victims of abuse are often unable or unwilling to complain to police; (2) many incidents are difficult to prove beyond a reasonable doubt; and (3) victims who make complaints may suffer retaliation.

Both the *Criminal Code* and the provincial guardianship laws provide elderly persons with some protection from neglect by requiring those responsible to provide the necessities of life to elderly persons who cannot provide for themselves. This legislation, however, is not well suited to those situations of elder abuse that call for an emergency response.

In summary, it is apparent that existing laws are of limited utility in responding to the problem of physical abuse and neglect of the elderly. Gordon et al. (1986) emphasize that these laws, though useful, are inadequate in protecting the elderly from neglect and abuse, because they fail to facilitate and support preventive and protective efforts.

In addition to *Criminal Code* sanctions against theft and fraud, the common law provides redress against duress and undue influence in financial decision making. However, both the *Criminal Code* sanctions and the applicable common law tend to be reactive and offer little protection. Some of the potential problems may be avoided by the granting of a power of attorney before the elderly person becomes vulnerable to such pressures. On the other hand, the enduring power of attorney may easily be abused and exploited. Many safeguards have been developed in different jurisdictions to prevent misuse. However, these safeguards often conflict with the basic concept of providing individuals with a simple method of managing their financial affairs after they become incapacitated.

There are two basic legal responses to abuse of elderly persons in institutions: government regulation and tort law. Some jurisdictions, such as Ontario, have introduced mandatory reporting of abuse in nursing homes. In addition, some jurisdictions have established "rights" of residents. Both approaches, however, are of questionable effectiveness. Mandatory reporting presents many difficulties, as will be discussed in the next chapter, while "rights" are usually vague and thus unenforceable.

Tort law may also provide a safeguard, since it imposes liability on the facility for harm to the residents. Unfortunately, this solution requires that the resident, or someone on the resident's behalf, take legal action against the institution for damages.

Canadian guardianship legislation (with the exception of such legislation in Alberta, Saskatchewan, and Quebec) provides little help in dealing with elder abuse. The major problem with guardianship legislation is that it tends to adopt an "all or nothing" approach. The lack of provision for appointing guardians with limited powers and/or for temporary periods conflicts with the principle of using the less intrusive alternative. Second, guardianship legislation offers protection only to incompetent persons for whom applications are brought forward.

The next chapter reviews special adult protection legislation that goes beyond those existing laws that afford protection to vulnerable adults in Canada.

CHAPTER 4

SPECIAL ADULT PROTECTION
LEGISLATION

The term *protective services* refers to a system of preventive, supportive, and surrogate services for vulnerable adults, and may encompass a wide range of social and community services (Regan 1983; Gordon et al. 1986). The legal framework for the provision of these services is often scattered among a variety of social welfare and health related statutes. However, following the model of child welfare legislation, many jurisdictions in North America have introduced special adult protection legislation, which was specifically designed in response to the problem of elder and/or adult abuse, and which creates considerable powers of investigation and intervention.

Protection legislation generally falls into one of three categories: (1) adult abuse legislation with mandatory reporting; (2) elder abuse legislation with mandatory reporting; (3) adult or elder abuse legislation with no mandatory reporting (Krauskopf and Burnett 1983; Lee 1986).

Forty-three jurisdictions in the United States currently have adult protection legislation, including 38 with mandatory reporting requirements (Lee 1986; Lewis 1986). With the exception of three states, these statutes have all been introduced since 1977. As Lee notes, "[s]eldom has a specific kind of legislation received such popular support and been enacted so quickly" (1986, 724).

Three Canadian provinces have had adult protection legislation for a number of years. The first was Newfoundland in 1973 (*Neglected Adults Welfare Act*, S.N. 1973, c. 81), followed by New Brunswick in 1980 (*Child and Family Services and Family Relations Act*, S.N.B. 1980, c. C–2.1), and Nova Scotia in 1985 (*Adult Protection Act*, S.N.S. 1985, c. 2) (Bissett-Johnson 1986; Gordon et al. 1986; Robertson 1987; Hughes 1988; Poirier 1988). In addition, in May 1988, Prince Edward Island passed the *Adult Protection Act*, S.P.E.I. 1988, c. 6. The Act came into force on December 1, 1988. The underlying aim of this type of legislation is highlighted in section 2 of the Nova Scotia legislation:

> The purpose of this Act is to provide a means whereby adults who lack the ability to care and fend adequately for themselves can be protected from

49

abuse and neglect by providing them with access to services which will enhance their ability to care and fend for themselves or which will protect them from abuse or neglect.

Like the legislation in most U.S. jurisdictions, the legislation in the Atlantic provinces is based on the child welfare model, and establishes extensive powers of investigation and intervention. These powers are discussed below. However, for the purposes of a general overview, the Nova Scotia statute is a useful illustration. The Act imposes a duty on every person to report to the Minister of Social Services any information indicating that an adult is in need of protection. The Minister is given broad powers of investigation and assessment, including the power to have the adult examined by a physician. If the Minister is satisfied that there are reasonable and probable grounds to believe that the adult is in need of protection, an application may be made to the Family Court for a protective intervention order. In cases of immediate danger, the Minister can authorize the removal of the adult to a place of safety without a court order. If the court is satisfied that the adult is in need of protection, and is not mentally competent to decide whether to accept assistance or is refusing assistance because of duress, it can authorize the Minister to provide protective services (including placement in a facility). The court can also order any person who is a source of danger to the adult to leave the premises where the adult resides, and can prohibit or limit that person's contact with the adult (Bissett-Johnson 1986; Gordon et al. 1986; Robertson 1987; Hughes 1988; Poirier 1988).

CHILD WELFARE MODEL

The adoption of the child welfare model in developing legislation to deal with elder abuse has been widely criticized (McLaughlin 1979; Katz 1980; Faulkner 1982; Note 1983; Gordon et al. 1986, 1987; Lee 1986; Metcalf 1986). Many view its adoption as a hasty, ill-considered reaction. As one author points out:

> Once a problem such as elder abuse is recognized by policymakers and legislators, the tendency is to find a quick solution. The elements of the elder abuse problem, however, are varied, delicate, and complex. [Note 1983, 377]

To some extent it is understandable why so many jurisdictions should have been willing to transplant the child welfare model into the field of elder abuse. Child welfare legislation is already in place and offers a convenient solution. Child and elder abuse may appear simply as different facets of the same problem — domestic violence. However, these similarities are superficial and misleading, and are apt to produce an inappropriate response to the problem of elder abuse. This is especially true of the concept of mandatory reporting. As Lee notes:

Mandatory reporting laws for suspected incidents of child abuse are based on three assumptions: (1) children are incompetent, helpless, and vulnerable; (2) children are at the mercy of their caretakers; and (3) society has a protectible [*sic*] interest in their children. The premise of these statutes is that the state, acting in its role as *parens patriae*, must protect those who cannot speak for or protect themselves. Instituting elder abuse reporting statutes based on such a premise implies that elders are incompetent and are unable to make a report on their own. Such an implication may serve to infantilize the elder's position in society, thereby furthering a form of bigotry towards elders known as ageism. [D. Lee, "Mandatory Reporting of Elder Abuse: A Cheap but Ineffective Solution to the Problem," *Fordham Urban Law Journal* 14 (1986): 730-31. Reproduced with permission.]

The critics of the child welfare model have focused particular attention on the requirement of mandatory reporting. This concept is considered in detail below.

ADULT ABUSE OR ELDER ABUSE?

In the United States, approximately half of the state legislation is directed at "elder" abuse, which is usually defined as involving individuals over the age of 60 or 65. The legislation in the other states applies to persons over the age of 18, but is often restricted to those suffering from physical or mental impairment (Sloan 1983; Lee 1986; Lewis 1986; Metcalf 1986).

Intervention legislation that focuses on age, rather than on incapacity to protect oneself from abuse, has been criticized by several writers for its promotion of ageism (Katz 1980; Faulkner 1982; Lewis 1986). They stress that age alone cannot justify interfering with an individual's right to self-determination, nor should an individual's refusal of services (particularly in cases of self-neglect) automatically give rise to a presumption of incapacity.

Some of the more recent legislation in the United States has attempted to address these concerns. For example, the District of Columbia *Adult Protective Services Act 1984*, D.C. Code Annotated (1989 Replacement), 6–2501, states that protective services will be provided only if three conditions are satisfied. First, the individual must be over the age of 18 and, because of physical or mental impairment, must be highly vulnerable to abuse, neglect, or exploitation. Second, the individual must currently (or in the recent past) be experiencing abuse, exploitation, or neglect by another person. Third, the abuse, neglect, or exploitation must be likely to continue because of the lack of anyone willing and able to provide adequate protection for the individual. The Act also provides that, in cases of self-abuse or self-neglect, protective services will be provided only if the self-abuse or self-neglect generates further abuse or neglect by another person (Lewis 1986).

The legislation in Minnesota adopts a similarly restrictive definition. A "vulnerable adult" is one who is at least 18 years of age and who is resident in a long-term care facility or who, regardless of residence, is unable or unlikely to report abuse or neglect without assistance because of impairment of mental or physical functions or emotional status (Note 1983; Ontario Ministry of the Attorney General 1987).

Canadian legislation is directed primarily at adult abuse and neglect, and is not limited to elders. The term "adult" is defined in such a way as to mean someone who is not a "child" for the purposes of the child welfare legislation. Thus, in Nova Scotia and Newfoundland, adult means a person aged 16 years or older; in New Brunswick the prescribed age is 19 (Robertson 1987). In the recent P.E.I. legislation, adult means a person who has attained the age of majority. However, the scope of these statutes is limited, as it is in many U.S. jurisdictions, by reference to physical or mental impairment. For example, the Nova Scotia legislation, in paragraph 3(b), defines an "adult in need of protection" as an adult who:

> (i) is a victim of physical abuse, sexual abuse, mental cruelty or a combination thereof, is incapable of protecting himself therefrom by reason of physical disability or mental infirmity, and refuses, delays or is unable to make provision for his protection therefrom, or
> (ii) is not receiving adequate care and attention, is incapable of caring adequately for himself by reason of physical disability or mental infirmity, and refuses, delays or is unable to make provision for his adequate care and attention.

New Brunswick is the only province that distinguishes between adults and elders. The New Brunswick legislation, like that in Nova Scotia, focuses on neglect and abuse caused by physical or mental infirmity, but in each case the victim must either be a disabled adult *or* an "elderly person" (which is defined as someone aged 65 or older) (Gordon et al. 1986; Poirier 1988).

In reference to the Canadian legislation, Gordon et al. state that "this response has been rather hasty and it has been the target of considerable criticism" (1987, 150). Several authors have criticized the legislation for the vagueness of its terminology, for example, a person "who is incapable of caring adequately for himself" (Sharpe 1983; Bissett-Johnson 1986; Gordon et al. 1986). Bissett-Johnson suggests that the definition of an "adult in need of protection" in the Nova Scotia legislation is "potentially so wide that it may catch every petitioner in an uncontested divorce based on physical or mental cruelty" (Bissett-Johnson 1986, 274). Gordon et al. take the view that the legislation is "riddled with value judgments embodied in vague terms, that allow a wide discretion by professionals" (1986, 57). They note, however, that the vagueness inherent in the Atlantic provinces' legislation is mitigated by policy guidelines that outline the criteria for intervention in much greater detail.

It is significant that the Prince Edward Island legislation contains much more precise (and restrictive) definitions of terminology and criteria. For example, it provides, in paragraph 1(i), that:

> "in need of protection" in relation to a person, means requiring legally authorized protective intervention in order to preserve essential security and well-being, the necessity for which arises because, owing to physical or mental infirmity or disability or other incapacity to remedy the situation himself, the person in need, being an adult, continually or repeatedly
> (i) is a victim of abuse or neglect by, or otherwise put in danger by the behaviour or way of life of, someone having recognized supervisory responsibility for the person's well-being,
> (ii) is incapable of fending for himself and is unable to make provision for necessary care, aid or attention, or
> (iii) refuses, delays or fails to arrange for or comply with necessary care, aid or attention.

MANDATORY REPORTING

Mandatory reporting of elder abuse was endorsed by the U.S. House Select Committee on Aging in its report on elder abuse issued in 1981. The Committee concluded that mandatory reporting was warranted because a significant number of the nation's elderly were probably victims of some form of abuse, and elder abuse was less likely to be reported voluntarily than child abuse (Lee 1986). The proposed federal legislation based on the Committee's report would have established a National Center on Elder Abuse to collect, conduct, and publish research on elder abuse, and would have provided federal funding to states that have mandatory reporting laws (Note 1983; Oakar and Miller 1983). Lee (1986) notes that, although the proposed legislation was not implemented, it appears to have had a significant effect on individual states in influencing them to introduce mandatory reporting legislation. Thirty-eight states (and the District of Columbia) now have mandatory reporting requirements (Lee 1986; Lewis 1986).

In most jurisdictions in the United States, the legal obligation to report cases of elder abuse is imposed only on certain individuals, usually health care professionals, social workers, and the police, with the medical profession being the group most often required to report (Sloan 1983; Lee 1986). This appears to be based on the view that physicians will often be in the best position to observe, recognize, and report symptoms of suspected physical abuse (Kapp 1982; Palincsar and Cobb 1982). Lee suggests that if the duty to report is imposed on the public as a whole, the effectiveness of the legislation will be diminished, since there is a danger that "everybody's duty may easily become nobody's duty" (1986, 740).

The reporting requirement in U.S. statutes is normally couched in terms such as "reasonable" or "probable" grounds for believing that an individual is the victim of abuse (Lee 1986). For example, the District of Columbia legislation requires a report to be made when the individual has "substantial cause" to believe that a person is the victim of abuse or neglect and is in need of protective services (Lewis 1986). In many U.S. jurisdictions, lawyers are exempt from the mandatory reporting requirement in recognition of the concept of solicitor-client privilege (Lee 1986; Lewis 1986).

In order to encourage individuals to report, the legislation in the United States normally grants the individual immunity from civil and criminal liability in the event that the report is unfounded. This protection from liability can take the form of either absolute immunity or immunity only if the person acted in good faith (Lee 1986).

In Canada, the introduction of mandatory reporting has been recommended by a number of writers (Gordon et al. 1986; Bristowe 1987) and by various committees and organizations, including the Ontario Advisory Council on Senior Citizens (1986), the Manitoba Council on Aging (Shell 1982), and the Review of Advocacy for Vulnerable Adults in Ontario (Ontario Ministry of the Attorney General 1987). The latter group viewed the absence of such legislation in Ontario as "startling" and recommended that its implementation be given the "highest possible priority" (Ontario Ministry of the Attorney General 1987, 153).

Newfoundland and Nova Scotia both have mandatory reporting provisions in their adult protection legislation. Unlike that in many American jurisdictions, the reporting requirement is not limited to specific groups or professionals. Every person who has information (whether or not it is confidential) indicating that an adult is in need of protection is required to report that information to the Director or Minister. Immunity from liability is given to persons who report information, unless the report is made maliciously or without reasonable and probable cause (Gordon et al. 1986; Robertson 1987).

New Brunswick does not have a mandatory reporting requirement, but its introduction is being actively considered (Gordon et al. 1986). The new legislation in Prince Edward Island provides for voluntary, rather than mandatory, reporting.

Recent amendments to Ontario's *Nursing Homes Act*, R.S.O. 1980, c. 320, have introduced mandatory reporting in respect of residents in those facilities. This is discussed in greater detail in Chapter 3.

Penalties

In the United States, the penalty for failing to report suspected cases of elder abuse ranges from a fine of between $25 and $1,000 to a maximum term of imprisonment of six months (Lee 1986). In addition, some jurisdictions provide that health care professionals who fail to report are guilty of unprofessional conduct and are subject to discipline by their professional bodies (Lewis 1986).

In Nova Scotia, the maximum penalty is a fine of $1,000 and one year imprisonment; in Newfoundland, it is $200 and two months' imprisonment. Ontario's *Nursing Homes Act*, R.S.O. 1980, c. 320, imposes a fine not exceeding $5,000 for the first offence and not exceeding $10,000 for each subsequent offence.

There also exists the possibility of civil liability for harm caused by a person's failure to report suspected elder abuse. There are cases in the United States in which damages have been awarded against physicians and others for failure to report cases of child abuse, and the same principle would likely apply to failure to report elder abuse in breach of a mandatory reporting requirement (Katz 1980; Palincsar and Cobb 1982; Trail 1985; Lee 1986; Metcalf 1986).

Effectiveness

A number of studies have cast doubt on the effectiveness (i.e., increased detection) of mandatory reporting in the context of child abuse (Katz 1980; Faulkner 1982). Many cases of child abuse go unreported despite mandatory reporting legislation. The same doubts have been raised in relation to the effectiveness of mandatory reporting of elder abuse. Studies in the United States indicate that the vast majority of reports of elder abuse and neglect are made on a voluntary basis by concerned citizens (Katz 1980; Faulkner 1982; Lee 1986; Metcalf 1986). For example, several studies have shown that reports of cases of elder abuse had already been known to social agencies or other officials (Block and Sinnott, 1979; Hickey and Douglass, 1981; Faulkner 1982). In the Block and Sinnott study, 95 percent of the cases had already been known to social agencies. Another study reported that the respondents in states with mandatory reporting laws typically did not believe that the reporting law had increased the number of reports (Alliance/Elder Abuse Project 1983).

Salend et al. (1984) compared 16 state elder abuse reporting statutes and analysed their implementation. The statutes failed to ensure consistent information about elder abuse, and the information that was collected was meagre. The available evidence suggested that neglect was more often reported than abuse, and within the neglect category, self-neglect predominated. These findings are consistent with another study that found disproportionately more self-neglect cases reported in the mandatory demonstration project (Hwalek 1988). In contrast, the Models Project found that more physical abuse reports occurred in the mandatory reporting model when compared to two other models (Wolf 1986).

Other studies examining the effects of mandatory reporting have suggested that there is a link between mandatory reporting and institutionalization of the abuse victim (Faulkner 1982; Crystal 1986). Faulkner's (1982) study in Connecticut found that 60 percent of those persons receiving short-term medical care would likely be institutionalized. However, it is debatable whether mandatory reporting leads to institutionalization. Contact with protective services may be an alternative explanation. In short, it appears that mandatory reporting laws are being passed in the absence of any evidence of their effectiveness. As Metcalf (1986) notes, if the effectiveness of mandatory reporting is in doubt, the intrusion on individual privacy is indefensible.

The effectiveness of legislation that places primary responsibility for reporting on the medical profession is also questionable, in the light of studies indicating that many physicians are reluctant to report suspected cases of elder abuse (Kapp 1982; Palincsar and Cobb 1982). As Kapp notes:

> [I]gnorance of legal reporting requirements is high. Further, those physicians who are cognizant of their legal duties still decline, in large numbers, to become involved in the legal intervention aspects of elder abuse. This may be . . . because physicians are generally uncomfortable with, and resistant to, legal issues and legal processes, perceiving such matters to be foreign to their healer role and exclusively belonging within the turf of the legal profession. Physicians may also shy away from an active involvement in elder abuse situations for fear of alienating the victim's relatives, who may be the perpetrators of, or the tacit accomplices to, the victimization. [M.B. Kapp, "Promoting the Legal Rights of Older Adults," *Journal of Legal Medicine* 3 (1982): 402-3. Reproduced with permission.]

One study found that, in a state that required physicians to report, only 2 percent of the reports originated from this source (Alliance/Elder Abuse Project 1983). Another study in two states that required mandatory reporting (i.e., Michigan and North Carolina) found that 71 percent of physicians surveyed did not know whether their state required mandatory reporting of elder abuse and 12 percent held the belief that reporting was not required (Crystal 1987).

Lee (1986) suggests that a community education program, coupled with a voluntary reporting system, is probably at least as effective as mandatory reporting legislation. A number of other authors and organizations have stressed the importance of public and professional education in attempting to solve the problem of elder abuse. These include such organizations as the Ontario Advisory Council on Senior Citizens (1986), the Manitoba Council on Aging (Shell 1982), and the Alberta Senior Citizens Secretariat (Stevenson 1985).

Criticisms and Problems of Mandatory Reporting

Many writers have questioned the wisdom of adopting mandatory reporting in the context of elder abuse. In particular, the following criticisms have been advanced. First, mandatory reporting is an inappropriate solution if the support services are lacking or inadequate (Katz 1980; Faulkner 1982; Shell 1982; Lee 1986). Without the necessary support services, mandatory reporting (even if effective) is at best nothing more than "case finding," and at worst is simply legislating for the sake of appearances (Faulkner 1982; Lee 1986). As Lee notes:

> Creating new legislation without funds to ensure its effective operation is not a solution to any problem. Simply passing a mandatory reporting law will not solve elder abuse. [1986, 752]

Many authors argue that intervention is justified only if the state has the capacity to offer something better (Staudt 1985; Crystal 1986; Moore and Thompson 1987). In the United States, the argument is that there are not enough health and social services currently available, and to institute mandatory reporting will place more of a strain on existing services. To create a separate response system would be a wasteful duplication and would be very costly (Crouse et al. 1981; Douglass and Hickey 1983). Mandatory reporting therefore raises the prospect of a solution that perhaps cannot be delivered, because most legislation has made no allowance for additional services. Without the services that help to maintain older people in the community, institutionalization is likely to be the only alternative (Chappell et al. 1986).

Mandatory reporting may also have a negative impact on the doctor-patient relationship, undermining the concepts of trust and confidentiality essential to that relationship. In many U.S. jurisdictions, the legislation expressly provides that the physician's obligation to report exists notwithstanding physician-patient confidentiality. A similar provision is contained in the Newfoundland and Nova Scotia legislation and in the Ontario *Nursing Homes Act*, R.S.O. 1980, c. 320. As a result, the abused elder may be discouraged from seeking medical assistance (Faulkner 1982; Palincsar and Cobb 1982; Krauskopf and Burnett 1983; Lee 1986; Metcalf 1986). Faulkner points out that:

> In addition to the invasion of the confidential relationship, the interference is worsened by the nature of the "service" likely to be offered. The report is likely to trigger an embarrassing investigation including the interviewing of friends and neighbors, and may result in removal of the elder person to an institutional setting and/or commencement of guardianship proceedings, stripping that person of many of his/her rights. The older person often, quite rationally, considers such a fate worse than the alleged abuse. [L.R. Faulkner, "Mandating the Reporting of Suspected Cases of Elder Abuse: An Inappropriate, Ineffective and Ageist Response to the Abuse of Older Adults," *Family Law Quarterly* 16 (1982): 84. © 1982 American Bar Association. Reprinted by permission of the American Bar Association.]

It has also been suggested that mandatory reporting may reinforce and encourage ageism in society (Faulkner 1982; Krauskopf and Burnett 1983; Lee 1986). Mandatory reporting is based on the premise that the victims of elder abuse are unable to seek help for themselves. Many critics question that premise, and emphasize that one should not assume that older people will not seek assistance if it is available (Faulkner 1982; Lee 1986; Metcalf 1986). Katz (1980) argues that, even if victims are reluctant to report elder abuse, it does not necessarily follow that others should be required to do so. She points out that the victim's reluctance may reflect a personal choice ''that it is better to stay in a situation that is less than satisfactory than to suffer the consequences of professional intervention'' (Katz 1980, 711; see also Lee 1986). Faulkner concludes that:

> The push for mandatory reporting therefore would appear to be a reflection of the attitude that old persons, like children, need more assistance and guidance, whether or not they know it or even want it. Policy planners and legislators should adopt, only with the greatest reluctance and demonstrated need, if at all, legislation which will further infantilise the older person. [Faulkner 1982, 87]

Lastly, it is significant that mandatory reporting is generally not utilized outside the context of child abuse, for example, in cases of spouse abuse (Faulkner 1982; Metcalf 1986). Metcalf notes that, although approximately one-fifth of elder abuse is spousal abuse, it has never been seriously suggested that battered spouses be institutionalized or forced to defend their competency at guardianship proceedings; nor are there mandatory reporting provisions to detect spouse abuse. Metcalf concludes that a response similar to that used in spouse abuse and other domestic violence laws, one that stresses crisis intervention, shelters, and counselling for both abuser and abused, might better protect the elderly while respecting their civil rights and allowing them greater self-sufficiency. This view is echoed by the Alberta Civil Liberties Research Centre (1988):

> Whatever is done to alleviate the problem, it must not be forgotten that there are significant differences between abused elders and abused children, even though both are dependent on others to a certain extent for care. Adults are presumed competent under the law and expect confidentiality in their communications with physicians and often other caregivers. Responses similar to those used in spousal abuse may be more appropriate, i.e., crisis intervention, shelters and counselling for the abuser and the abused. These may better protect individuals while respecting civil rights and allowing elders greater self-sufficiency. [Alberta Civil Liberties Research Centre 1988, 115]

TYPES OF INTERVENTION AND MANDATED POWERS

Adult protection legislation in the United States contains a wide range of powers of intervention. As Regan (1981) notes:

> Protective services programs are rarely limited to clients who voluntarily accept their services. The legislative scheme often provides for the use of guardianship or conservatorship by the protective agency to ensure that the client accepts the assistance that the caseworker believes is necessary. Some states also have created special court procedures to secure court orders

for protective services, for placing the client in an institution, for emergency orders when there is imminent danger to the client's health or safety, or for orders authorizing entry into an uncooperative client's home. [Regan 1981, 1113]

Particular concern has been expressed at the power to remove the individual to an institution. A number of writers emphasize that greater care should be taken to ensure that the removal is for a short term only, because of the inherent danger of long-term institutionalization. For example, studies of the system in Connecticut indicate that 60 percent of individuals removed for ''short-term medical care'' do not return home (Faulkner 1982; Krauskopf and Burnett 1983).

The more recent trend in the United States appears to be towards restricting the scope of the powers of intervention in cases where the individual withholds consent to protective services. Jurisdictions such as Florida and the District of Columbia have recently revised their protective services legislation, with emphasis now being placed on providing services to those who want them and to those who, because of incapacity or fear and intimidation, are either unable or unwilling to consent (Lewis 1986; Metcalf 1986).

In the Atlantic provinces, adult protection legislation creates extensive powers of investigation and intervention (Bissett-Johnson 1986; Gordon et al. 1986; Robertson 1987; Hughes 1988; Poirier 1988). Although the four Atlantic statutes use different terminology and criteria, the legislative schemes are essentially the same. Once a report of suspected abuse or neglect is received, social or community services personnel conduct an investigation and an assessment, which may include an examination by a physician. The legislation in New Brunswick expressly provides that the physician may conduct the examination without the adult's consent. If either the adult or the person having custody and control refuses to cooperate, an application can be made to the court for a warrant to conduct the investigation.

Following the assessment, if the adult is considered to be in need of protective services, these can be provided on a voluntary basis. Alternatively, an application may be made to the court to have the adult declared to be in need of protection. The court has a number of powers that it may exercise. In Newfoundland, the court can order that the adult shall: (1) remain in his or her residence subject to supervision by the Director of Neglected Adults; (2) be removed to the home of some suitable person and be committed to the care and custody of that person; or (3) be committed to the care and custody of the Director, who may place the adult in a home or institution. Similar provisions are contained in the legislation of New Brunswick, P.E.I., and Nova Scotia. In these provinces, however, because the statute is directed at abuse as well as neglect, the court is given additional powers. It can issue an order against any person who is a source of danger to the adult, requiring that person to leave the premises where the adult is living, or prohibiting or limiting that person's contact and association with the adult.

In one important respect, the Nova Scotia legislation differs from that in other Atlantic provinces. A court can declare an adult to be in need of protection only if it is satisfied that the adult is not mentally competent to decide whether to accept the assistance of the Minister, or is refusing the assistance by reason of duress. The Nova Scotia legislation attempts to place emphasis on voluntary assistance, with involuntary intervention being viewed as a last resort (Gordon et al. 1986). A recent report on the New Brunswick legislation recommended that the Act be amended so as to make mental incompetency a prerequisite of an intervention order (New Brunswick Special Committee on Social Policy Development 1989).

In Nova Scotia, P.E.I., and New Brunswick, an order of the court expires after six months unless it is renewed. There is no equivalent provision in the Newfoundland Act. The legislation in all four provinces provides for a right to apply for a variation of the order, and a right of appeal (Gordon et al. 1986; Robertson 1987).

The strong parallel between the Atlantic provinces' legislation and child welfare legislation is evident not only from the legislative scheme itself, but also from the way in which it has been interpreted by the courts. The courts have taken the position that their approach to adult protection legislation should be essentially the same as in child protection hearings. The court must first be satisfied that the adult is in need of protection, as defined in the legislation, and then it decides what type of order would be in the adult's best interests (Robertson 1987).

The legislation in Prince Edward Island contains many of the powers found in the legislation of the other Atlantic provinces. One significant difference, however, is that the P.E.I. Act attempts to link the responses to elder abuse with the concept of guardianship, an approach that is often found in legislation in the United States. Section 15 provides that, where a person in need of assistance or protection is evidently unable to make reasonable judgments necessary for his personal welfare or affairs, and it seems likely that the incapacity will remain for a period of time beyond the time when decisions should in the person's best interests be made, the Minister may apply to the court for the appointment of a guardian. Provision is also made for the appointment of a temporary guardian (for up to 30 days) when there is considerable risk of serious harm to the adult or to the adult's estate.

CHARTER IMPLICATIONS OF SPECIAL LEGISLATION

Existing Due Process Requirements

As Gordon et al. note:

> Resolving the conflict between, on the one hand, the demand for due process protections and, on the other, the need to avoid complex, formal, stigmatizing, and often expensive judicial proceedings which are counter-productive to the health and welfare needs of the elderly, is a key problem area. [1986, 108]

Adult protection legislation in the United States has been severely criticized for its lack of due process safeguards (Regan 1981, 1985; Kapp 1983; Sloan 1983; Gordon et al. 1986). Both Regan and Sloan describe the standards for intervention as "vague and conclusory," and note that there are serious procedural flaws in the laws of several states. They also point to the lack of accountability once the court has signed the order, and charge that protective services (especially when provided by a public agency) are becoming a mechanism that allows the public agency to assume total domination over elderly clients. Regan is particularly critical of the use of protection legislation as a means of institutionalizing an individual while circumventing the procedural and substantive safeguards contained in the mental health and guardianship legislation.

It is noteworthy that those jurisdictions that have recently introduced or amended their adult protection legislation have tended to include detailed due process requirements. Indeed, in some cases, the primary purpose of recent amending legislation has been to provide for greater safeguards to the elderly person's rights during investigation and hearings. For example, the legislation in the District of Columbia contains a wide range of due process requirements, including the right to notice, the right to legal representation, and the right to present evidence and cross-examine witnesses (Lewis 1986). Similarly, Florida's 1986 statute was designed to facilitate the investigation of abuse and the provision of services by the least restrictive alternative, while providing greater protection for due process (Metcalf 1986).

The absence of meaningful due process provisions in the legislation in the Atlantic provinces is the subject of detailed criticism by Gordon et al. Referring to the Newfoundland legislation, they observe that:

> The adult who is allegedly "neglected" must be notified of a hearing and also of any hearing to vary or rescind an order. However, the adult is not explicitly granted any due process rights at such hearings. Neglected adults may be compelled to undergo "treatment" in hospital and, through the combined effects of the powers set out in the statute, may be forcibly removed from their homes for this purpose, provided the criteria for neglect are present. . . . Certainly the Act makes provision for an appeal to the Supreme Court against any order, judgment, etc., (s. 16); however, this seems to be a weak protective provision. It does nothing to protect

fundamental rights and freedoms of the individual who is adjudged "neglected" and consequently subjected to certain dispositions without an opportunity to challenge the validity of the actions of a supposedly benign state. [R.M. Gordon, S.N. Verdun-Jones, and D.J. MacDougall, *Standing in Their Shoes: Guardianship, Trusteeship and the Elderly Canadian* (Burnaby, B.C.: Simon Fraser University, Criminology Research Centre, 1986), 45. Reproduced with permission.]

The criticism that Gordon and his associates make of the Nova Scotia legislation is even stronger. They note that the criteria for intervention are "vague in the extreme," and that there is a complete absence in the legislation of any due process rights, such as the right to legal representation. They conclude that "in Nova Scotia the issue of the right to self-determination is considered far less important than the right to protection," and describe the legislation as "Draconian" (Gordon et al. 1986, 45).

Gordon et al. also point out that policy makers and professionals in Newfoundland are having serious reservations about the "paternalistic over-reach" of the adult protection legislation. They note the irony that as one Atlantic province (Newfoundland) begins to question the utility of the statute, another (Nova Scotia) introduces almost identical legislation.

The Review of Advocacy for Vulnerable Adults in Ontario, also known as the O'Sullivan Review (Ontario Ministry of the Attorney General 1987), recognized the difficulties inherent in adult protection legislation, and the need to find an appropriate balance between paternalism and respect for autonomy. Interestingly, however, it felt that the Nova Scotia legislation had achieved that balance. It noted that:

> It is obvious that the enactment of protective legislation for vulnerable adults is not free from complexity; there must be reasonable alternative residences available to which the abused can be removed; the removal of vulnerable adults from their homes is contrary to the current social policy of promoting deinstitutionalization and reducing the warehousing of the vulnerable; and some abused adults would prefer to endure their home circumstances rather than accept the alternative of removal to an institution, however safe. Fortunately, there are a number of precedents of adult protection legislation in jurisdictions in the United States and in other provinces which have dealt with these issues. For example, Nova Scotia and Minnesota have developed effective enactments to address these concerns. [Ontario Ministry of the Attorney General, *You've Got a Friend: A Review of Advocacy in Ontario*. Report of the Review of Advocacy for Vulnerable Adults (Toronto: Queen's Printer, 1987), 150. © Reproduced with permission from the Queen's Printer of Ontario.]

The O'Sullivan Review concluded that the Nova Scotia legislation could be "readily adapted to the Ontario context" (Ontario Ministry of the Attorney General 1987, 153). However, the protective legislation envisaged by the O'Sullivan Review, unlike the Nova Scotia statute, would be closely linked to the expanded advocacy system, with an advocate being assigned in every case to provide independent monitoring and to facilitate reporting of subsequent abuse.

The legislation in Prince Edward Island makes some attempt to ensure due process protection. It provides that the adult in respect of whom an order is sought has the right to be heard, with legal counsel, at any proceeding, and has the right to have legal representation provided at the expense of the Minister if that expense is beyond the means of the adult. The Act also provides that, in any application for a protective intervention order, the onus lies with the Minister to prove that the least intrusive and restrictive option practical is being sought.

The Canadian Charter of Rights and Freedoms

The lack of due process safeguards in Canadian adult protection legislation is of particular concern in light of the *Canadian Charter of Rights and Freedoms* (1982). Gordon et al. (1986) state that there can be little doubt that current adult protection legislation in Canada will have to be revised to comply with the *Charter*. Indeed, this is probably true of Canadian guardianship laws in general (Gordon et al. 1986; Gordon and Verdun-Jones 1987; Robertson 1987; Savage and McKague 1987; Hughes 1988). The extent to which adult protection legislation encroaches upon personal liberty and autonomy has been emphasized by many writers (Katz 1980; Faulkner 1982; Gordon et al. 1986; Hughes 1988; Poirier 1988). Clearly there is a need for proper due process protection and precise criteria if the legislation is to comply with the *Charter*.

Section 7 of the *Charter* provides that:

> Everyone has the right to life, liberty and security of the person and the right not to be deprived thereof except in accordance with the principles of fundamental justice.

Section 15(1) provides that:

> Every individual is equal before and under the law and has the right to the equal protection and equal benefit of the law without discrimination and, in particular, without discrimination based on race, national or ethnic origin, colour, religion, sex, age or mental or physical disability.

Hughes (1988) suggests that the effect of the *Charter*, and in particular of sections 7 and 15(1), is probably that any adult protection legislation must reflect the philosophy of the least restrictive alternative. She also states that, since the term "fundamental justice" in section 7 of the *Charter* has been interpreted by the Supreme Court of Canada as involving substantive and not just procedural fairness, compelling reasons would have to be present to justify the deprivation of a person's liberty and security pursuant to adult protection legislation.

Section 15(1) is of particular concern in relation to protection legislation based on age *per se*, as opposed to mental or physical inability to protect or care for oneself. As is noted above in section 6.2, many writers have criticized protection legislation in the United States as promoting ageism and discrimination. In order to comply with section 15(1) of the *Charter*, legislation would have to be based on proven vulnerability rather than on age. For example, the age limit found in the New Brunswick legislation, discussed above, might well be held to be a contravention of section 15(1) of the *Charter*.

The legislation in Nova Scotia has recently been the subject of challenges under the *Charter*, with mixed results. In *Nova Scotia (Minister of Community Services)* v. *Carter* (1988), 89 N.S.R. (2d) 275 (Fam. Ct.), White J.F.C. held that the *Adult Protection Act* does not violate the *Charter*. However, in a more recent decision — *Nova Scotia (Minister of Community Services)* v. *Burke* (1989), 91 N.S.R. (2d) 413 (Fam. Ct.) — Niedermayer J.F.C. held that the scheme of the Act is so unbalanced and uncompromising as to be contrary to the *Charter*.

CONCLUSIONS

Forty-three jurisdictions in the United States and four jurisdictions in Canada have enacted some type of adult protection legislation. This type of legislation has, to a large extent, been modelled after child welfare legislation. However, the similarities between child welfare issues and elder abuse are superficial and misleading. Thus, the enactment of adult protection legislation has been characterized by much controversy and criticism.

First, intervention legislation that uses the criterion of age rather than incapacity to protect oneself from abuse has been labelled as ageist. Critics of this definitional age approach stress that age alone cannot justify interference with an individual's right to self-determination.

Second, most jurisdictions with adult protection legislation in the United States and Canada have included a mandatory reporting requirement. It is somewhat surprising that mandatory reporting is so popular, since it may involve an intrusion on an individual's privacy (e.g., in the context of a doctor-patient relationship), and there is a lack of evidence indicating that it is effective in increasing identification of abuse or as a deterrent to abusers.

The most common characteristic of adult protection legislation is that it contains a wide range of powers of intervention. Many jurisdictions have given their protection services the power to remove individuals to institutions. However, there has been a recent trend in the United States to restrict this power, particularly when the potential "client" withholds consent.

Adult protection legislation has been severely criticized for its lack of safeguards for due process. In Nova Scotia, for example, the criteria for intervention are vague and there is an absence of concern for due process. In such jurisdictions, the right to self-determination seems to be less important than the right to protection.

The lack of due process safeguards in Canadian adult protection legislation is of particular concern in light of the *Canadian Charter of Rights and Freedoms*. The extent to which adult protection legislation encroaches upon personal liberty and autonomy as defined in sections 7 and 15 of the *Charter* has been the topic of considerable concern.

While the aim of adult protection legislation may be laudable, the means adopted to achieve this end must impair as little as possible the rights and freedoms of the individual. The criteria for intervention must be precisely defined. They must be based on vulnerability rather than on age alone. Due process rights, such as the right to notice and the right to legal representation, must be respected. Above all, the legislation must truly reflect the principle of the least restrictive alternative if it is to withstand scrutiny under the *Charter*.

CHAPTER 5

REVIEW OF PROGRAMS AND SERVICES

Service programs for adults have two primary characteristics: (1) actual or potential legal authority to provide substitute decision making for the client; and (2) the administration and coordination of delivery of services to adults at risk (Regan 1983). The legal authority of adult service programs may fall under adult protection acts (e.g., in Florida, District of Columbia, Prince Edward Island); however, this is not always the case. For example, some adult services or services for the elderly may fall under hospital or nursing home legislation or may be established without legislative authority, as in the case of informal advocacy programs.

In terms of the administration and coordination of the delivery of services, a program provides a blueprint for service delivery, establishes resources, and coordinates actual service delivery through direct government service provisions or through private or public agencies. Programs are responsible for ensuring that clients are provided with whatever services they need in a coordinated, effective, and efficient manner (Ontario Ministry of the Attorney General 1987).

The general functions of programs include: (1) determination of policy goals and objectives; (2) assessment of client needs; (3) development of a comprehensive plan for service delivery; (4) arrangement for direct service delivery; (5) assessment of service delivery; and (6) evaluation and follow-up.

With regard to adult protection,

> [a] protective services program combines a multitude of services and draws on nearly every resource available to elders in any given community . . . [a] protective services program is a unique mixture of legal, medical, and social services that permit the broadest array of interventions. [Quinn and Tomita 1986, 235]

Services provide direct support and assistance to clients in a variety of ways. Adult service programs coordinate numerous services designed to meet the general needs of vulnerable adults and the elderly. Such services may include, for example, home care services, home-maker and nursing services, and senior citizen housing services. The review of the literature, as well as interviews with key experts, has revealed that very few existing services are specialized for, or strictly limited to, providing protective services for victims of elder abuse. Several states and provinces have 24-hour hot lines and a few have temporary emergency shelters, but there appear to be few specialized services available beyond these.

In this chapter, three general types of programs will be discussed. First, programs that fall under the adult protection approach similar to the child welfare model (identified in Chapter 4) will be examined. Generally, these are statutory adult protection service programs that are mandated by adult protection legislation. Second, programs attached to the family violence model will be examined; and, third, advocacy programs for the elderly will be discussed. Following the discussions of the adult protection, family violence, and advocacy programs, the client services available through these programs will be examined. It is important to note that, regardless of what approach is followed, the same services tend to be utilized.

ADULT PROTECTION PROGRAMS

As outlined in Chapter 4, the adult protection approach is characterized by special powers of investigation and intervention, and mandatory reporting. The intervention strategies associated with adult protection programs may include the power of removal, and compulsory custody and services.

In 1975, Title 20 of the *Social Security Act* in the United States mandated and funded protection service programs for all adults 18 years old or older (Quinn and Tomita 1986). In response, a majority of states established their own adult protection legislation, and many states developed adult protection service programs. These programs relied either upon social service agencies or upon services delivered by public or private agencies contracted with the Title 20 funds.

With the passage of adult protection legislation in the Atlantic provinces, protective services were delivered through the provincial departments of social services. For example, Nova Scotia established a specific program called the Adult Protective Services Unit within the provincial social services department. The purpose of Adult Protective Services was to provide protection for adults (16 years of age and older) who were physically disabled and/or mentally infirm and therefore unable to care for themselves.

At present, Adult Protective Services in Nova Scotia are primarily concerned with crisis intervention. The program refers clients to direct services, which vary greatly from community to community. The circumstances of the particular case and the resources available in the community in which the incident occurs determine what services are used. Emphasis is placed on bringing services into the home; again, this depends greatly on the services available in the community. Institutionalization is viewed as a last resort, although it may be a viable option in some cases.

The recently passed Prince Edward Island legislation used the Nova Scotia Act as a model, but it does not include mandatory reporting. It contains a 68-step implementation plan that incorporates a multidiscipli-nary response to reported cases of elder abuse. It appears to be a very thorough approach, intended to utilize as many different resources as are required in each particular case.

There are no specialized services for elderly victims of abuse or neglect in Prince Edward Island. However, two departments, Health and Social Services and Home Care and Support, are currently developing the Adult Protection Program. This program will involve coordinating already exist-ing services, such as home care, nursing, occupational therapy, and home-maker services.

A review of the adult protection service programs in Canada and the United States indicates that the nature and organization of protective ser-vices may vary considerably among jurisdictions, depending on the legis-lation mandating the programs as well as the existing local resources (Hobbs 1976; Zborowsky 1985; Quinn and Tomita 1986). Adult protec-tion service programs combine a multitude of services requiring collabo-ration and cooperation among a number of agencies. In many cases, the adult protection service worker, who may be mandated by adult protec-tion laws, must coordinate the agencies involved in direct service provi-sion. The worker must follow established legal guidelines and criteria that often include: provisions for geriatric evaluations; voluntary protective services; involuntary court-ordered protective services; court hearing and petition procedures; mandatory reporting of abuse; and appeal mechan-isms (Zborowsky 1985). The clients served can be voluntary or involun-tary, neglected or self-neglected, abused or abusive (Quinn and Tomita 1986).

Much of the controversy surrounding adult protection service programs is a direct result of modelling them after child protection service programs (Crystal 1986; 1987). The most significant issues appear to be: (1) the appropriateness of an enforcement-oriented approach to service provi-sion; and (2) the inherent contradictions in the system that become evi-dent through implementation. Both issues are discussed briefly below.

The legal intervention role assigned to practitioners in the enforcement aspect of adult protection service programs has been subject to consider-able scrutiny. The proponents of mandated intervention are careful to state that the individual rights of the older person must be safeguarded and his or her individual level of functioning enhanced (Bookin and Dun-kle 1985; Staudt 1985; Zborowsky 1985; Quinn and Tomita 1986; Girard 1988). They argue that little can be done for the abused adult victim who refuses services unless the practitioner wishes to place himself or herself at legal risk (Sharpe 1988). However, it has been suggested that practi-tioners, without legal support, may lack the confidence and willingness to intervene. To challenge the competency of an older adult's ability to care for himself or herself, or to accuse a family member of maltreatment of his or her loved one is a serious accusation (Girard 1988).

In addition, adult protection workers have been criticized as "trigger-happy" when it comes to petitioning for guardianship in order to place older persons in nursing homes (Mitchell 1979; Quinn and Tomita 1986). The argument is also made that, because the caregiver is burdened by caring for the older person, protective services intervention functions to relieve stress on the part of the caregiver. In doing so, however, the victim is restricted and, as a result, loses control and privacy (Quinn and Tomita 1986). Finally, opponents to the legal intervention approach note that the intervention infantilizes the older person — who is treated the same way as are children under child welfare legislation (Pillemer 1985b; Crystal 1986).

The inherent contradictions of adult protection services programs have become evident with their implementation (Hobbs 1976; Bookin and Dunkle 1985; Guinn 1985; Staudt 1985; Zborowsky 1985; Hayes et al. 1986; Matlow and Mayer 1986; Quinn and Tomita 1986). Given the vagueness of the legislation and the lack of protocols in some jurisdictions, adult protection workers are in a quandary in terms of deciding what constitutes abuse. Thus, balancing the two conflicting principles of *parens patriae* or right to protection and the right to privacy is a constant struggle (Quinn and Tomita 1986). Using legal powers to force oneself into an older person's home and, at the same time, attempting to respect that person's right to privacy borders on the impossible. While collaboration and teamwork are required in the delivery of adult protection services, the adult protection worker, as well as other agency workers involved in the delivery of service, can share little information for reasons of confidentiality. Also, the potential for conflict among service providers is high. For example, a lawyer will defend a client from judicial intrusion, whereas a social worker is likely to seek judicial sanction for changing the client's situation (Quinn and Tomita 1986; Anderson 1989). Unfortunately, until more information is collected through program evaluations, the arguments and problems associated with the adult protection approach will continue to be based primarily on anecdotal evidence and speculation.

DOMESTIC VIOLENCE PROGRAMS

The domestic violence model is only now being considered as an alternative to the child welfare model because it does not violate people's rights nor does it discriminate on the basis of age (Crouse et al. 1981; Faulkner 1982; Finkelhor and Pillemer 1984; Pillemer 1985b; Crystal 1987). Because the domestic violence model has primarily served as an example with which the child welfare model has been compared, there has been little thereotical development of the model, very few services representing the approach have been implemented, and as would be anticipated, few evaluations of service effectiveness have been made.

The domestic violence model involves crisis intervention services, a strengthened role for the police, court orders for protection, emergency and second-stage sheltering, support groups for the abused and the abuser, and the use of a whole range of health, social, and legal services. An integral component of domestic violence services is public education and education of the abused about their rights (Crouse et al. 1981).

To date, there are several individual and group programs for victims of elder abuse. The Victim's Services Agency in New York has instituted support and consciousness-raising groups for victims of elder abuse. Senior centres in Winnipeg and Calgary offer individual counselling for abused older people, as do a few women's emergency shelters (Ghent et al. 1985). Several states have special shelters for older abuse victims (Cabness 1989) and several women's shelters do house older abused women (MacLeod 1987). Most attempts at service delivery have been sporadic and have shown no evidence of coordination. The ''newness'' of the model for dealing with elder abuse may account for these observations.

The difference between spouse abuse and elder abuse when neglect is considered to be part of the definition can be problematic (Crouse et al. 1981, 7). Police intervention, restraining orders, and education about rights are senseless in the face of family or self-neglect.

The spouse abuse model is not without its critics (Schechter 1982; Walker 1984; Beaudry 1985). There are problems with police response (McDonald et al. 1986), with restraining orders (MacLeod 1987), with shelters (Beautry 1985), and with follow-up services (Sample Survey and Data Bank, University of Regina 1984). To illustrate, in one Canadian study, 42 percent of the women were still harassed by their abusers despite restraining orders; police response was very low and sometimes non-existent in emergencies; and follow-up services were not easily obtained because of transportation problems, access problems, and financial barriers (McDonald et al. 1986). More to the point, Podnieks et al. (1989, 14) uncovered the fact that 32 percent of elder abuse victims were ''not very aware'' or only ''somewhat aware'' of public legal services (assuming they were effective). The empirically substantiated flaws in the domestic abuse model need to be closely examined before transferring them to the elder abuse field.

The gerontological research would caution against the singular use of crisis intervention, since older persons' problems tend to be multiple and interrelated, tend to take longer to solve, and need to be monitored closely (Ledbetter Hancock 1990). The question of who will oversee coordination of services is also raised after crisis intervention has occurred. Transfer trauma or relocation stress may be no less severe if an older person is moved to a shelter instead of a nursing home. The research on aging repeatedly shows that the help-seeking behaviour of older people is to turn to an informal network initially, to family and friends, and to contact agencies and professional service organizations as a last resort (Gourash 1978; Chappell et al. 1986; Connidis 1989). This preferred behaviour of older persons may preclude the effective use of the domestic violence model.

ADVOCACY PROGRAMS

In the broadest sense, advocacy refers to those activities that involve speaking for or acting on behalf of an individual or a group in order to ensure that their needs are met and their rights are respected (Ontario Ministry of the Attorney General 1987). The advocacy approach recognizes that the older person is an adult in a potentially vulnerable position (Crouse et al. 1981; Hwalek 1988).

Advocacy assumes that the least restrictive and intrusive appropriate intervention will be used in assisting victims of abuse, neglect, and exploitation. If the victim of abuse has an advocate to assist in guaranteeing protection of rights and obtaining goals, existing community structures and services can be used for protection. In practice, advocates can inform clients of their rights and the alternatives to service, and can assist in carrying out agreed-upon plans. An important feature of this approach is the advocate's independence from the service delivery system. Advocates have the opportunity to establish a positive relationship with clients, since they do not represent the intrusive aspects of the state or the police (Crouse et al. 1981).

In attempting to define advocacy, it is important to differentiate between legal and social advocacy, as well as between formal and informal advocacy. Legal advocacy is the best-known type of advocacy and refers to the representation provided by a lawyer for a client in court. Legal advocacy includes preliminary activities, such as negotiation and settlement, that may keep a dispute out of court.

The concept of non-legal or social advocacy has been defined by the Ontario Review of Advocacy for Vulnerable Adults as follows:

> Similar to legal advocacy, social advocacy means speaking or pleading on behalf of others and entails many of the same professional responsibilities: for example, an assessment of the situation; advising the client and assisting him or her to decide upon the best course of action; and using one's skills and best efforts to pursue the client's wishes through all lawful, ethical and reasonable means. The basic difference, however, is that a social advocate speaks or pleads on behalf of another by using non-legalistic measures: he or she, unlike a lawyer, does not directly invoke or participate in the legal process to obtain the desired result. [Ontario Ministry of the

Attorney General, *You've Got a Friend: A Review of Advocacy in Ontario*. Report of the Review of Advocacy for Vulnerable Adults (Toronto: Queen's Printer, 1987), 40–41. © Reproduced with permission from the Queen's Printer for Ontario.]

The O'Sullivan Review (Ontario Ministry of the Attorney General 1987) also distinguished between informal and formal advocacy. Informal advocacy takes place on a relatively unstructured and voluntary basis, involving, for example, family members or relatives, friends, neighbours, and volunteers. Self-advocacy, which involves acting on one's own behalf, is also included as a type of informal advocacy.

Formal advocacy is performed by individuals who are paid for providing advocacy services, and may be mandated by legislation. Formal advocacy programs are structured, and are characterized by special goals, membership, leadership, and financial support of some kind. A number of formal advocacy programs found in Ontario are discussed below. These include two social advocacy programs and one legal advocacy program.

A number of formal social advocacy programs already exist in Ontario. One is the Psychiatric Patient Advocate Office (PPAO). Established in 1982, the PPAO provides advocacy services to patients in the ten provincial psychiatric hospitals. Its mandate includes the investigation of alleged incidents and the assessment of institutional and systemic responses to these incidents (Turner et al. 1984; Atkinson et al. 1985; Manson 1987; Ontario Ministry of the Attorney General 1987). The Manson Committee has recently completed a comprehensive external evaluation of the PPAO and has made detailed recommendations for its improvement (Manson 1987).

The Adult Protective Services Program (APSP) is a case management program that also contains a social advocacy component.[1] Its mandate includes advocating on behalf of its clients as well as on behalf of developmentally handicapped adults in general. The inclusion of both case management and advocacy responsibilities is a difficult task (Ontario Ministry of the Attorney General 1987; Savage and McKague 1987).

An example of a formal legal advocacy program that is of particular relevance to the elderly is the Advocacy Centre for the Elderly (ACE). This was established in 1984 as a specialized legal aid clinic serving the needs of the elderly in Toronto. In 1985–86, it provided advice to over 2,000 individuals and referred approximately 1,500 inquiries to other agencies. The ACE is concerned primarily with legal advocacy, including providing legal advice to the elderly and representing them before courts and tribunals (Gordon et al. 1986; Ontario Ministry of the Attorney General 1987).

There are few American examples of advocacy that deal directly with elder abuse. The Connecticut program with the state Ombudsman would be an excellent example if not for the fact that mandatory reporting is required (Walker 1983).

The program proposed by the Illinois Department of Aging is one of the more sophisticated approaches in the United States. It is based on voluntary reporting, since it is considered to be the least restrictive response to elder abuse. Intervention is to be approached from a family systems perspective, and any older person is to have access to an advocate regardless of income. Self-neglect is omitted from the definition of abuse because it was felt this could be handled through regular channels. Participants must have attained 60 years of age, a criterion which is consistent with other gerontological programs. It is recommended that enabling legislation for the administration of the program include immunity from liability for persons reporting abuse situations and for those assessing the reports. The Department of Aging would utilize the existing network in implementing the program. Necessary enhancements to the current service system include standardized assessment procedures, intensive casework, systematic follow-up, and some supplemental services not readily available, such as emergency services. Public and professional education on elder abuse is a key aspect of the program and is believed to be at least as effective as mandatory reporting (Hwalek 1988).

Advocacy programs can also direct attention to elder abuse in institutions without using mandatory reporting. The Consumer Advocate for Better Care in North Central Massachusetts is an independent organization with a board of directors (mainly professionals) and 14 paid advocates for the elderly (Stathopoulos 1983). Advocates monitor the quality of care in area nursing homes by visiting each of the nursing homes frequently, often unannounced, and at varying times, including evenings and weekends. The advocates initially explain their role and the procedures they use for problem resolution to nursing home administrators. They receive complaints directly from residents and also maintain a hot line on which complaints may be registered anonymously. Advocates frequently talk with staff and read patients' charts. Detailed records are kept of every complaint and its resolution. This information has been used for community education and for influencing public policy (Stathopoulos 1983).

Hooyman (1983) proposes the use of natural helping networks by professionals as a means to detect and prevent elder abuse. She reviews the existing gerontological programs that have been used to deal with other problems experienced by the elderly and makes a case for their use in responding to elder abuse. Support programs for families experiencing stress can easily incorporate information about elder abuse and can be used as screening mechanisms to detect abuse. Older people can be provided with information about elder abuse through almost any existing programs, such as self-growth, health, pre-retirement planning programs, leisure programs, and clubs. Volunteers in phone-a-friend, adopt-a-grandparent, friendly visiting, buddy systems, widow-to-widow, and neighbourhood watch programs could be trained in the detection and reporting of elder abuse. Mail carriers, utility workers, and "handicab" personnel could also be trained in detection. Professionals and paraprofessionals would also require training. The Council on Aging of Ottawa-Carleton has, for example, designed an elaborate educational model to help organizers of information sessions explain the nature of elder abuse to different types of audiences (Labarge 1988).

Although ombudsman programs in nursing homes are becoming more popular, few empirical assessments of the programs are available (Monk and Kaye 1982; Zischka and Jones 1984). There have been examples of using nursing home resident councils as advocates for residents; however, the one extant study showed that residents had very little control over this mechanism (Devitt and Checkoway 1982). The Council on Aging of Ottawa-Carleton surveyed 88 Ontario institutions and community settings about institutional policies concerning elder abuse, data collection procedures, protection of rights, and staff educational programs (Council on Aging of Ottawa-Carleton 1987). They received 55 completed questionnaires from community-based agencies and centres, including health services, community resource centres, and social service agencies. The results indicated an absence of policy and protocol for dealing with suspected cases of elder abuse in institutions and agencies serving elderly clients. On the basis of these findings, the Council on Aging proposed educational models for older adults, community, family, and professionals. The objectives of these models include: (1) creating awareness of the problem of elder abuse; (2) developing the content and tools for presentation of this information; (3) collecting and disseminating research material; and (4) motivating the community to contribute to the development of mechanisms to address the problem of elder abuse (Council on Aging of Ottawa-Carleton 1988).

Advocacy undoubtedly plays an important role in protecting and furthering the interests of vulnerable adults. In many respects Ontario has been at the forefront in Canada in establishing advocacy services. However, an extensive review of existing services found them to be less than adequate. The O'Sullivan Review described the present system as fragmented and concluded that:

> [t]he gaps in the present system produce inequities and discrimination. Vulnerable adults in some care facilities receive advocacy services from dedicated volunteers and others may receive quality advocacy if they are fortunate to be assigned care providers who are committed to advocating on behalf of their clients. Regrettably, the majority of our vulnerable adults and particularly those residing in smaller communities do not have access to any advocacy programs. [Ontario Ministry of the Attorney General 1987, 5]

REVIEW OF SERVICES

The preceding sections reviewed the three major types of programs — adult protection programs, domestic violence programs, and advocacy programs — that currently respond to elder abuse. It is not useful to categorize the services by a similar trichotomy, since at least two of the program approaches use the same services (adult protection and advocacy programs). The major criteria for choosing a particular service depend on the nature of the individual case and the resources available. Since domestic violence programs have been rarely used by older persons, there are few services to evaluate.

The literature indicates that services attached to programs are mainly drawn from existing service systems designed to serve the general needs of the elderly. The only difference between the models appears to be who, if anybody, coordinates the services. For example, in adult protection programs, it appears that the protection services worker coordinates services (Quinn and Tomita 1986). In the advocacy approach, it appears that the advocate coordinates service delivery (Hwalek 1988). Most service programs draw upon all forms of care from both the public and the private sectors and use various funding mechanisms to pay for these services.

In both Canada and the United States, the spectrum of services for older persons covers a wide variety of care needs. These services include community support services (home-makers, senior centres, meals-on-wheels, etc.), multifacility or multifunction living and care complexes (senior citizens' housing), congregate or sheltered housing (foster homes, lodges), long-term care facilities (nursing homes and auxiliary hospitals), medical care (hospitals) and socio-medical care (day hospitals, respite care, adult day care) (Chappell et al. 1986). A continuum of care is implied in these services, ranging from integrative adjustment services (pre-retirement counselling, leisure activities, education) and supportive services (co-ordinated legal, medical, psychiatric, and social services) to specialized terminal care facilities and services (Beattie 1976; Coward 1979; Chappell et al. 1986). In both Canada and the United States, the ultimate goal seems to be to use the least restrictive alternatives possible and to maintain older persons in their own homes (Kammerman 1976).

It is important to note that the health and social service systems for older persons in Canada are very different from those in the United States. Canadian programs are more likely to be universal (e.g., medical care), to be based on need rather than on age, and to be uniform rather than based on income differences (Chappell et al. 1986). Most importantly, the global concept of health (social-psychological) is more evident in Canada compared to the predominantly medical approach in the United States. In terms of service delivery, this means that in Canada there is a better likelihood of using medical services for medical-social needs. Lastly,

Canada tends to have more extensive public programs than the United States (Weller and Manga 1982).

In the light of the differences between the American and the Canadian literature on service delivery for older persons, it appears that the American findings may not be directly transferable to the Canadian context. All of the American studies on elder abuse indicate a lack of services, particularly within the area of home care and the need for emergency housing (Wolf 1986; Hwalek 1988). The problem of arranging payments for some ancillary services was also frequently noted. These factors would not be as problematic in those provinces (e.g., Manitoba) with integrated, universal, free-to-consumers home care programs. In the other provinces, however, some mechanism for coordination, such as an advocate, would be necessary. In those provinces where some ancillary services are not presently covered or are attached to medical assessments (e.g., Newfoundland), difficulties with payment could be solved by including the costs in the elder abuse program.

Although there are general differences between Canada and the United States, it is also important to note differences between provinces in the coordination of home care and what is included in the services (Forbes et al. 1987). For example, British Columbia, Manitoba, and Saskatchewan successfuly coordinate home care and community support systems that include home-maker services, home nursing, therapy services, medical services, social workers, meals-on-wheels, and household repair services. Other provinces, which offer these services on an *ad hoc* basis, have experienced coordination problems. Because of these coordination problems, some provinces are now considering the "single entry system" as in Alberta or the "One-Stop Access" program in Ontario, wherein an older person is screened at the front end of all services. Once the person is screened, a long-term plan that is overseen by a single case manager is put in place (Committee on Long Term Care for Senior Citizens 1988).

Existing research on the evaluation of services available to the elderly is extremely limited. In fact, only three substantial studies are presented in the literature: (1) the Benjamin Rose Institute Study; (2) the Models Project in Massachusetts, New York, and Rhode Island; and (3) the Elder Abuse Demonstration Program in Illinois.

The Benjamin Rose Institute Study was a controversial study carried out in Cleveland in the early 1970s. An experimental research design was used to test the effectiveness of protective services. Older persons referred to the project were randomly assigned to either the control group or the experimental group. The control group received the usual community services available to older people. In contrast, the experimental group received casework as a core service plus seven ancillary services supposedly of the finest quality and unlimited in quantity (Blenkner et al. 1974). It was hypothesized that the experimental group would have higher contentment scores and survival rates than the control group.

Contrary to the predicted outcome, the findings showed that the institute's specialized protective services were not more effective than the ordinary community services. The most significant long-term outcome was a higher rate of mortality for the experimental group. Apparently, the social service intervention resulted in the placement of more of the experimental clients in nursing homes, and these placements resulted in a higher mortality rate — an outcome that is often associated with institutional placement (Blenkner et al. 1974). The findings were so controversial that the data were reanalysed in 1981 using more sophisticated statistical procedures.

The 1981 reanalysis clearly identified the flaws in the original design that were responsible for the controversial findings (Dunkle et al. 1983). For example, the use of mortality and institutionalization rates as decisive indicators of program effectiveness is highly questionable. In addition, there are serious problems associated with the non-random assignment of caseworkers to the two experimental groups, as well as the merger in the analysis of two non-equivalent experimental groups. Lastly, there was insufficient documentation of services to differentiate between services provided to the control group and to the experimental group (Dunkle et al. 1983). The reanalysis strongly supports the claim that these factors contaminated the original research to the extent that conclusive inferences cannot be drawn.

The Models Project in three Eastern states evaluated three models of protective service delivery (Wolf 1986). The three models represented different approaches for providing services to the abused elderly and intervention that include: (1) the service brokerage model; (2) the coordination model; and (3) the mandatory model. However, a close reading of the project indicates that the actual differences were primarily organizational. The service brokerage model was located in a single agency that had the authority and capacity to deliver all required services; the coordination model involved a coordinator of services supplied by other agencies; and the mandatory model was a mixture of both, controlling some of its own services but also relying on community services. It is interesting to note that the last model included mandatory reporting at the time of the study.

Three criteria were selected to measure the success of the three different models: (1) case resolution; (2) community response; and (3) project replicability. Data were collected from case assessments at both intake and case closure. In addition, data were collected from two community surveys, one conducted at the beginning of the grant period and the other two years later.

All three projects reported a decrease in the number and the severity of manifestations of abuse and neglect of clients at the time cases were closed. The most effective strategy for all three models was a change in social or living situations; the least effective was a change in the circumstances of the abuse (Wolf 1986). Resolution was more apt to be identified with persons who were more dependent and neglected than with those who were less dependent and physically maltreated.

The community surveys showed that the services used most by the projects were services for the elderly, social agencies, home health organizations, and the police. The most needed service at all sites was an emergency shelter, and the most mentioned training need was information about local resources. The second survey showed that community agencies had come to rely on the demonstration projects to deal with abuse and neglect.

From an organizational perspective, the brokerage model, based on case management, took longer than the other models to deliver services, and workers did not rate client outcomes more favourably. It did, however, receive the highest rating from community agencies. The mandatory model, which was a mix of the other two, received the lowest rating because of poor coordination and overall performance. Whether or not mandatory reporting had any relation to the evaluations is not clear. The report concludes that the coordination model was the easiest to replicate, although fewer than half of the community agencies rated its performance as excellent (Wolf 1986).

The Elder Abuse Demonstration Program in Illinois compared two advocacy programs, an adult protection (child welfare) program, and a legal program primarily relying on criminal offence provisions. Evaluation was carried out by a number of firms and, although it was sophisticated in design, there were many inconsistencies across sites. At the end of the project, it was not possible to ascertain which program was more effective, because the caseworkers tended to be similar in the way they provided direct service; that is, they all used the casework approach (Hwalek 1988). This may account for the reporting of very few differences among the three models for programs. Notwithstanding the design problems, the study reported that the adult protection program spent more time on public education, while the advocate programs spent much more time assisting people to make decisions. The most frequently used services at all sites were in-home health services, in-home assistance, adult day care, and home-delivered meals.

Overall, the findings of the studies are very limited. It is impossible to tell which program, if any, is better, since only the Benjamin Rose study even considered that issue. Interestingly, and regrettably, none of the studies considered the client's perspective.

A less debated, but equally important, issue is whether elder abuse is best responded to categorically, through legislation and programmatic solutions centred directly on the abuse problem, or whether it is best seen as a problem to be addressed mainly by more generic health and social services (Callahan 1982, 1988; Crystal 1986; Wolf 1986). Presumably, those in favor of a specific response to elder abuse would argue that the hidden nature of the problem, its scope, and the lack of services (especially in rural areas) demand a specific categorical response. Wolf (1986) questions whether abuse services would be better located in age-segregated or age-integrated agencies, while Crystal (1986; 1987) speculates whether special abuse services are required at all.

At the heart of the issue is the notion of ageism, discussed in Chapters 3 and 4. The dangers of ageism — dependency, stigmatization, and separation — have been well documented in the gerontological literature (Estes 1979; Dowd 1980; Guillemarde 1980; Townsend 1981).

A second consideration is whether elder abuse typically exists as a relatively self-contained problem that can be addressed on its own terms or whether it represents a single dimension of a more complex problem (Douglass and Hickey 1983; Crystal 1986). Experience with protective services suggests that abuse is only one component of a larger network of complicated problems. To focus only on the abuse dimension can unbalance a complex social, psychological, and economic equilibrium that has taken a lifetime to develop (Crystal 1986). Furthermore, a singular focus on elder abuse creates an artificial split in the services already available to meet similar, related needs (Crystal 1986).

The gerontological literature suggests that treatment interventions are more effective when delivered through those agencies that already serve the elderly (Zimberg 1978). The workers in these agencies are supposedly in the best position to recognize problems, they are familiar with services for the aged, they understand the complexities of the older person's problems, and the context is less stigmatizing for the older person.

CONCLUSIONS

The lack of data about the nature, extent, and outcomes of elder abuse has made it difficult to plan, implement, and evaluate effective social remedies (Pillemer 1985b; Crystal 1987). Nevertheless, professional and political interest in elder abuse and the concomitant pressure to ameliorate the problem have spawned a wide variety of programs and services for elderly persons in need of protection.

The adult protection approach has been perceived as having the most potential for violating the rights of older persons, while the advocacy approach has been viewed as having the least potential for rights violations. Mandatory reporting, investigation, and intervention can very quickly and easily override the rights of the older person, but so can police intervention, especially when police have the power to lay charges irrespective of the abused person's wishes. Reporting, whether it is mandatory or not, will still result in an investigation or an attempt at an investigation. In short, all adult protection programs are potentially intrusive. If there is to be a response to elder abuse, the scope and severity of the problem will have to be weighed against the degree to which rights are to be violated. Further, possible built-in safeguards should be considered.

The legislation behind the adult protection approach has been seriously criticized as a manifestation of ageism, since age-specific provisions have been stated in the absence of an acknowledgement of judgemental impairment. According to the definitions of ageism, this is a valid observation. This criticism, however, could also be relevant to the advocacy programs. To provide an advocate for persons over 60 years of age on the basis of law is a form of age discrimination. Theoretically, the practice of ageism is difficult to avoid if there is to be a categorical response to the problem of elder abuse.

Domestic violence programs serve the general population and may not totally meet the needs of the elderly. Neglect is a category of mistreatment that would not be served by domestic violence programs; crisis intervention may not be comprehensive enough; the effect of moving older persons into shelters is unknown; and all of the problems identified in service delivery to abused spouses would likely pertain.

The effectiveness of informal advocacy and its link with organized, formal advocacy in the case of elder abuse is unknown. Again, there are descriptions of programs but no actual evaluations.

Available findings point to three significant issues that should be considered when developing advocacy systems. First, the fragmentation of the current advocacy system should be taken into account in the development of an advocacy program for adult protection service delivery. The O'Sullivan Review (1987) suggests that additional measures should be taken to address the vulnerable adult problem (e.g., protection legislation); however, a comprehensive, centralized advocacy program that serves as a focal point for a particular jurisdiction might be equally effective.

Second, the focus of the advocacy approach should be considered. In some jurisdictions, the question of whether advocacy should include systemic as well as individual advocacy is a major issue.

Last, although advocacy may appear to be non-intrusive, in practice it can be quite intrusive, especially if the advocates are immune from liability and are not accountable. The temptation to forge ahead, contrary to the older person's wishes, could exist if the advocate is not held responsible in some way.

The service issues relevant to both adult protection and advocacy programs are: (1) which services should be provided; (2) who should be responsible for delivering these services; and (3) what type of organizational format should be adopted. It is evident from the literature that the services already available to older persons provide the resources used in response to elder abuse, regardless of which approach is utilized, and new or unique services are not necessarily required. However, the variation in types and availability of services in different communities is a serious problem that must be addressed. The major challenge appears to be one of accessing limited resources in critical or emergency situations. Modification and coordination of already existing social services for the elderly to ensure their ready accessibility was found to be a better remedy than the establishment of a new set of services.

The organizational patchwork of gerontological services, especially in the United States, has made coordination, collaboration, and follow-up somewhat difficult for practitioners operating under adult protection programs. The advocacy approach, with an advocate located outside the direct service delivery and case management systems, could provide an effective mechanism for calling on all types of services and ensuring their coordination and implementation from beginning to end. An advocate may also be in a better position to offer education to the public and to professionals, to identify gaps in the system, and to respond to institutional abuse.

NOTE

1. Although the name of this program would suggest that it is an "adult protection program" (see Chapter 4), the program does not include special powers of investigation and intervention.

CHAPTER 6

THE REALITIES OF DIRECT PRACTICE

The preceding chapters have outlined the definitional, theoretical, and methodological problems surrounding the issues of elder abuse and neglect. Unfortunately, these problems are not purely matters of academic interest but have critical implications for practitioners who encounter elder abuse and neglect in day-to-day practice. Indeed, the practitioner is in a very curious position, in which he or she is expected to solve a problem for which the definition is unclear; for which there are no reliable estimates of the people affected; for which there are no definitive causes; and for which intervention strategies are untested.

Given this paucity of knowledge, Montgomery and Borgatta, from their vantage point in academe, have expressed dificulty in understanding, ''. . . the rapid emergence in the literature of recommendations for practice and policy'' (1986, 599). From the vantage point of the practitioner, the answer is easy. The practitioner can hardly wait for new knowledge to be generated before attempting to ameliorate the abuse situations confronted in practice, nor can he or she ignore the law. In the absence of a well-developed body of knowledge the only alternative is to use the available knowledge while being acquainted with the controversies surrounding elder abuse and neglect (Phillips 1989, 92-93). It is from this perspective that many practitioners and several researchers have tried to develop guiding frameworks or protocols for screening for high risk, for assessment, and for intervention. In this chapter we examine these aspects of practice by reviewing the available protocols found in the elder abuse literature with the aim of highlighting the attendant problems for the practitioner.

IDENTIFYING WHO IS AT RISK

A number of practitioners and researchers have attempted to identify groups of older persons who are potentially at risk for abuse, neglect, or inadequate care. Presumably, the goals of high-risk screening are to sensitize the practitioner to what is considered to be a hidden problem (Kosberg 1988) and to take preventative measures before serious damage occurs (Breckman and Adelman 1988). To facilitate the task of identifying high-risk elders a number of screening devices have appeared in the elder abuse literature (Pillemer 1986; Quinn and Tomita 1986; Fulmer and O'Malley 1987; Sengstock and Hwalek 1987; Breckman and Adelman 1988; Kosberg 1988; Podnieks 1988; Hamilton 1989).

Most of the schemes include characteristics of the older person, characteristics of the caregiver, and depending upon the theoretical proclivities of the author, characteristics of the family system. There appear to be only several guidelines that consider the characteristics of the institution (Fulmer and O'Malley 1987; Pillemer 1988; Podnieks 1988). Some of the schemes, such as the Risk for Elder Abuse at Home (Hamilton 1989), seem to be more appropriate for domestic settings, while others, such as the set of indicators laid out by Fulmer and O'Malley (1987), are more appropriate for medical settings.

For illustrative purposes, one of the more thorough screening devices for risk is the High Risk Placement Worksheet (HRWP) developed by Kosberg (1988) contained in Appendix A. This instrument can be used generically to identify problems in the caregiving situation but also to prevent abuse. According to the author, the HRWP ''. . . allows for the systematic assessment of the quantitative and qualitative characteristics of the elderly person, major caregiver and the family system by a trained professional'' (Kosberg 1988, 48). The HRWP can be used in a preventative fashion before placing an older person into the care of his or her family or can be used to assess an already existing situation. The questions are asked independently of the caregiver and the older person, and when incongruities occur between the two sets of responses, the professional should explore further. An accumulative high-risk score rating is not the goal of the HRWP; it is simply a guideline for the professional.

As would be expected, the indicators in most instruments are directly traceable to the factors reportedly found to be associated with elder abuse (Chapter 1) and incorporate some of the more popular "theories" (Chapter 2). Herein lies the problem for the practitioner. In the first instance, almost all of the screening instruments contain many of the items that were found to be associated with abuse in the earlier, descriptive, and less rigorous studies of elder abuse. For example, Kosberg's first characteristic of the high-risk elder is female, but this characteristic has now been questioned by the exceptional study by Pillemer and Finkelhor (1988) of elder abuse, which found that the risk of abuse for elderly men is double that of elderly women. Similarly, there is growing evidence that the abused elder is *not* necessarily older or economically disadvantaged (Godkin et al. 1989); that the older abused person is *not* more impaired than the non-abused elder (Phillips 1983; Pillemer 1986; Bristowe 1987; Pillemer and Finkelhor 1989); that dependency is more a characteristic of the caregiver (Bristowe 1987; Anetzberger 1989; Godkin et al. 1989; Pillemer and Finkelhor 1989); and that intergenerational violence is *not* always the norm (Pillemer 1986; Godkin et al. 1989). While Kosberg's HRPW is relatively recent and quite useful, it has the potential to be misleading and is representative of most screening devices found in the elder abuse literature.

In the second instance, most of the configurations of risk factors are limited to the current stereotype that older persons are abused by their adult children, in the face of mounting evidence that a substantial proportion of elder abuse is actually spouse abuse (Hageboeck and Brandt 1981; Giordano 1982; Wolf et al. 1984; Pillemer and Finkelhor 1988; Podnieks et al. 1989). No current instrument for detecting high-risk candidates that was reviewed directed the practitioner to probe the past and the current state of the older person's marital relationship. Furthermore, in another analysis of the data gathered by Pillemer and Finkelhor between 1985 and 1986, it was found that the items that distinguished the abused group from the non-abused group were those pertaining to the abuser and his or her behavior and circumstances and not items pertaining to the older victim (Pillemer and Finkelhor 1989, 183). In the struggle between the competing theoretical frameworks of family violence versus caregiver stress, the screening items tend to favour caregiver stress, when in fact both positions are most likely viable (Sprey and Matthews 1989).

A related conceptual problem is that of distinguishing between the risk for abuse and the risk for neglect, a distinction absent in most protocols. There is some indication that the two processes are quite different in so far as neglect is not necessarily the first step on a continuum that automatically ends in abuse (Giordano 1982; Wolf et al. 1984; Pillemer and Finkelhor 1988; Hudson 1989). Pillemer and Finkelhor (1988) showed that living situation (living with a spouse and at least one other person) and gender (male) were associated with high risk for physical abuse, whereas neglected elderly persons tended to be in poor health and to report that they did not have close contacts on whom they could rely for help in time of difficulty (1988, 54). Most recently, Hudson (1989) has delineated the critical attributes of abuse and neglect and their empirical referents, which could be incorporated into most screening tools.

Finally, it is worth noting that most screening instruments have not been tested in terms of their ability to actually predict abuse and neglect, and the few that have exhibit several methodological and statistical problems. For example, Sengstock and Hwalek (1986), in their attempt to create a clinical screening device, did not have the luxury of starting with a random sample of older persons but used case files from nine different agencies. Hamilton (1989) established the criterion validity of the Risk of Elder Abuse in the Home (a Canadian instrument) by having six social workers compare their own subjective clinical assessment with their own use of the instrument over 120 trials of the form — which is to say that there was no independently defined criterion (1989, 25). While Kosberg (1988) stated that his scheme was based on the literature, he did not indicate whether or not it was clinically tested for its predictive ability.

By now, it should be obvious how the muddle in the elder abuse research can be transferred into practice. The outcome for the practitioner can be missing those at risk for abuse (married older persons) or taking discriminatory action against those who — for whatever reason — appear to fit the "scientific" profile of the abuser or the victim (any younger caregiver living with an elder) (Sprey and Matthews 1989). There is also the problem that the wrong services will be marshalled for the wrong people (home care services for the person at risk when job counselling services are required for the abuser).

If the best knowledge available is to be used for determining who is at risk for neglect and abuse, the work of Pillemer and Finkelhor has to be seriously considered. Their research comes closest to meeting the requirements for reasonable prediction in the context of violence research (Gottfredson and Gottfredson 1988, 304-05). While their study was not without flaws, random sampling was used; the population at risk was interviewed directly; the criterion variables were fairly reliable (the Conflict Tactic Scales for abuse and the Older Americans Resources and Services for neglect); base rates were established (frequency of the occurrence of the event); and the predictive ability of factors associated with neglect and abuse were actually tested (Pillemer and Finkelhor 1988; 1989). The Canadian Study (Podnieks et al. 1989) also meets these criteria, but the final report is not yet available.

The data of Pillemer and Finkelhor (1988) suggested that those at risk for neglect were in poor health and did not have close contacts to assist in times of difficulty. The configuration of those factors associated with abuse were: being male, living with a spouse and an adult child, and being in poor health (Pillemer and Finkelhor 1988, 54). In the case of caregiver abuse, the characteristics of dependence and deviance on the part of the abuser were more powerful predictors then characteristics of the potential victim; and in the case of spouse abuse, the characteristic of abuser deviance and the degree of spousal conflict were stronger predictors of abuse then characteristics of the potential victim (Pillemer and Finkelhor 1989, 185).

To summarize, the "state-of-the-art" in screening for neglect and abuse would strongly indicate that practitioners will have to proceed with considerable caution by not blindly following given protocols and by being flexible in the incorporation of the newer research as it becomes available. To date, the latest research is suggestive of a slight shift in focus to the characteristics of the potential abuser and to the nature of the marital unit when screening for risk. In turn, these factors may change, pending further research and clinical experience.

ASSESSMENT PROTOCOLS FOR NEGLECT AND ABUSE

A number of data collection instruments and protocols for assessment have been introduced into the elder abuse literature to identify abuse or neglect after the maltreatment has allegedly occurred. Assessment protocols not only heighten the practitioner's awareness of the problem but also serve the useful purpose of systematically guiding the practitioner through a series of symptoms that could be missed in sometimes confusing situations (Quinn and Tomita 1986; Fulmer and O'Malley 1987). An Ontario study also recommends that protocols should be somewhat standardized among agencies and institutions, presumably to provide information about the extent of the problem in a given geographical area (Council on Aging of Ottawa-Carleton 1987).

There are a number of approaches to assessment, which include checklists of the different types of abuse and/or indicators of abuse and neglect (Shell 1982; Ross et al. 1985; Sengstock et al. 1986; Breckman and Adelman 1988; Podnieks 1988; Fulmer 1989); a review of the victim's physical, psychological, social, medical, and support systems in conjunction with guidelines such as those set forth by governments (U.S. Department of Health and Human Services 1980; Falcioni 1982; Ferguson and Beck 1983; Phillips 1983; Quinn and Tomita 1986; Alberta Senior Citizens Secretariat 1987); and categories of situations believed to be associated with neglect and abuse (O'Malley et al. 1983; Fulmer and Cahill 1984; Fulmer and O'Malley 1987). Some assessment protocols use the above-mentioned procedures in combination and add standardized tests such as the Mini-Mental Status Exam (cf. Quinn and Tomita 1986). Several of the more detailed protocols, such as the Elder Abuse Diagnosis and Intervention Model developed by Quinn and Tomita (1986) or the Staircase Model developed by Breckman (Breckman and Adelman 1988) include possible intervention strategies and case management features. Lastly, several protocols, such as the Elder Assessment Instrument used at Beth Israel Hospital (Fulmer and O'Malley 1987), depend upon team assessments. The methods of data gathering range from professional subjective observations (Rathbone-McCuan and Voyles 1982) through the use of descriptive questions (Falcioni 1982; Sengstock et al. 1986) to Likert-type scaling of the severity of the maltreatment (Ferguson and Beck 1983). In Appendix B we provide, as an example, the data collection tool for assessment of elder neglect and abuse by Ross et al. (1985) for nurses. An aggregate of observations may alert the nurse to the possible diagnosis of abuse or neglect.

Most of the assessment protocols are based on the underlying assumptions found in the abuse literature on elders, children, and women. Most have incorporated the assessment processes employed by the helping professions, such as nursing, social work, medicine, and psychology

(Quinn and Tomita 1986). Not surprisingly, the protocols have certain flaws that originate with the inadequacies in theory development and research, and that are exacerbated by the realities of practice. Like the screening instruments, most assessment protocols focus on caregiver stress at the expense of exploring marital violence or socio-emotional maladjustment on the part of the perpetrator. To complicate matters, the abuse situation is rarely straightforward. Typically, the practitioner is faced with a situation wherein signs of damage are elusive, the intentions of the abuser are not readily apparent, it is difficult to attribute blame, and the victim is unwilling or unable to name the perpetrator (Phillips 1989, 87).

Some of the more vexing problems for the practitioner result from the narrow definitions of abuse and neglect that have made their way into assessment protocols (Fulmer 1989), for example: the confusion between indicators of risk and actual abuse (Sengstock and Hwalek 1987); the struggle to determine the basis of neglect (Fulmer and O'Malley 1987); the clouding of judgemental and objective data (Sengstock and Hwalek 1987); difficulties in administering protocols; and the lack of empirical support for assessment instruments.

According to Fulmer and O'Malley (1987) the definitions of abuse and neglect are too narrow to fully encompass the problems confronted by practitioners, although the authors do admit that there are no objective data to indicate how well the various definitions have worked in practice (1987, 20). Nevertheless, this problem is not unique to elder abuse and is typical of any written assessment procedure. The attempt to fit human beings into categories always runs the risk of what McLaughlin (1988) calls "reductionism"; that is, the immense complexity of the older person's life becomes overly simplified and treated as reality (McLaughlin 1988, 32). Making judgements about a client's mental competency according to a check-list in one or two meetings in a sometimes unfamiliar environment (an emergency ward) can produce inaccurate assessments and deleterious results for both the older person and the practitioner. Similarly, the complexity of the elder's intimate family interactions are rarely captured in a static assessment form.

In a project funded by the Administration on Aging, Sengstock and Hwalek (1987) examined seven elder abuse identification measures developed by various researchers and agencies (one was Canadian). Each instrument was separated into its constituent items and the items examined to determine the types of abuse measured. What they found was that more than half of the items (57.6 percent) were actually risk indicators and only 14.3 percent of the items dealt with actual indicators of physical abuse (Sengstock and Hwalek 1987, 24). While risk assessment is obviously important, more definitive symptoms of abuse are essential for determining the type of intervention required, especially in cases where legal intervention might result. They also found that there were very few items to measure the various forms of maltreatment other than physical abuse. For example, material abuse and psychological neglect were rarely measured in the instruments, increasing the probability that these conditions would be overlooked by the practitioner (Sengstock and Hwalek 1987).

Even when the signs for physical or psychological neglect are included in protocols, there is still the problem of disentangling the combination of effects resulting from normal aging processes, chronic disease processes, medications, and neglect (Fulmer and O'Malley 1987; Fulmer 1989). It is, of course, almost impossible to untangle these effects completely, but that does not mean they should be ignored in an assessment. As Fulmer (1989) illustrated, an indicator of persistent hunger could be a function of diabetes mellitus, poverty, lack of transportation, the drug Ritalin, or neglect. A review of the possible causes of a symptom can refine the assessment and increase the likelihood of choosing the appropriate intervention.

Few assessment protocols, however, direct the practitioner to consider systematically whether a symptom is the result of aging, a disease state, the social context, or medications before settling on a diagnosis of neglect. Although Fulmer (1989) has devised a means for evaluating signs of neglect, the procedure is noticeably absent in most assessment protocols. Attempting to make these kinds of distinctions in suspected cases of neglect is particularly important, since neglect is supposedly one of the most frequent types of maltreatment reported by practitioners (Salend et al. 1984; MacEachron et al. 1985).

In a related issue, the previously mentioned study by Sengstock and Hwalek (1987) discovered that many of the items in the assessment instruments relied on professional judgement rather than on the collection of objective data by the practitioner. Normally, a valid identification measure would focus on objective information to be subsequently used by the practitioner to make a judgement. As would be expected, the judgement process came into play most frequently when an attempt was made to discern psychological abuse and neglect. As an example, the item "deliberate inappropriate care" is subject to numerous interpretations (Sengstock and Hwalek 1987, 30).

The researchers also found that the practitioner had to make judgement calls about the accuracy of caregiver accounts and about caregiver intentions, since there were no items that measured these factors. While it has been argued that the judgement call of an experienced professional may cause few problems (Sengstock and Hwalek 1987), the research of Phillips and Rempusheski (1985; 1986) suggests otherwise.

In one of her earlier studies, Phillips (1983) found that when practitioners had relatively concrete guidelines upon which to base their decisions for the detection of elder abuse, they still classified cases incorrectly because they were influenced by other situational factors. Some of these factors were uncovered in an inductive study of 29 nurses and social workers who had, on average, eight years of work experience with older persons (Phillips and Rempusheski 1985). Although the definitions of abuse offered by the professionals reflected the generally accepted definitions for elder abuse, the factors actually considered in the diagnostic decision were quite different (Phillips and Rempusheski 1985, 135). In practice, the professionals decided about the nature of the "situation" according to the intentions of and the effort expended by the caregivers; the degree of cooperation in the relationship between the professional and the caregiver; the elder's attributes (helpless, difficult); and the acceptability of the reasons for the caregiver's acts (Phillips and Rempusheski 1986, 136-137). In an earlier analysis of the same data, the authors found that cultural stereotypes (ethnic background) and professional and personal values significantly influenced the decision to label a situation as abusive (Phillips and Rempusheski 1985). The most disturbing finding was that ". . . the gravity of the consequences for the elder was not considered in seeing the situation as abuse or neglect" (Phillips and Rempusheski 1986, 137).

Some of the difficulties in administering assessment protocols can be directly attributed to the realities found in practice. Access to the victim is a problem frequently reported by practitioners. Without access and the opportunity to observe behaviour as requested in many protocols, practitioners are forced to use other means, such as the telephone, for which there are few, if any, documented procedures (Sengstock and Hwalek 1987). Some protocols presume considerable knowledge about elder abuse and gerontology, and for a practitioner working outside his or her area of expertise an inappropriate protocol can simply cause more complications. To ask a community social worker to report on bedsores or a hospital nurse to uncover material abuse could result in questionable assessments (Sengstock and Hwalek 1987). Lastly, many assessment protocols do not have wide applicability (Fulmer and O'Malley 1987) in so far as they have been developed in isolation and tend to focus on the characteristic symptoms seen in an agency's specific caseload (Sengstock and Hwalek 1987). Not only do they defeat the purpose of standardizing assessment procedures, but the practitioner comes up short when attempting to apply an in-home assessment protocol to a nursing home setting where there are, for example, numerous caregivers and sometimes family involved.

Finally, very few of the assessment instruments or protocols have been rigorously tested clinically, so there is no way to determine if they facilitate the identification of abuse in a reliable fashion. The testing of the Elder Assessment Instrument (EAI) used at the Beth Israel Hospital is a rare exception. The hospital used the EAI to assess all persons 70 years of age presenting themselves at the emergency department and compared this group with the cases referred to the Elder Assessment Team, which also used the EAI. It was found that those cases referred to the Elder Assessment Team were more likely to receive a poorer rating on items related to clothing, hygiene, nutrition, and skin condition. They were more likely to have evidence of bruising, bedsores, or dehydration; were more dependent in their "lifestyle"; and were less interactive with significant others. There were no differences on the items for medical assessment (Fulmer and O'Malley 1987, 46-48). According to the researchers, the EAI continually undergoes revision for the purposes of improving clinical practice (Fulmer and O'Malley 1987). While it is tempting to suggest that the EAI is one of the better protocols available in the literature, it is important to note that it really measures inadequate care that *might* be abusive (Fulmer and O'Malley 1987) and that it was developed in a medical setting with access to a wide variety of professionals.

To be equipped with faulty assessment instruments or protocols for use in unclear circumstances is undoubtedly trying for the practitioner. On the basis of their research on nurses and social workers, Phillips and Rempusheski (1985) argued that diagnostic decision making exhibits many of the elements associated with the model for conflicted decision making. In their study, the practitioners' decisions concerning elder abuse were reportedly intense, involved unpleasant feelings of distress, were coloured by uncertainty and a reluctance to make irrevocable choices, and were complicated by the risks of utilitarian losses for both the practitioner (e.g., social disapproval) and the elder (e.g., loss of self-determination) (Phillips and Rempusheski 1985, 139). Given the confusion found in many of the current assessment instruments over what is measured, what is not measured, or whether anything is measured, and the mix-up between objective observances and judgements, it is not likely that the diagnostic decision-making process would become less onerous with an assessment protocol in hand.

In short, current assessment protocols are conceptually unclear; the items are poorly operationalized, confounding objective data with professional judgement; the protocols do not address some of the more pressing realities of practice; nor have they been empirically tested. This is not to say that they should be tossed aside, but rather that they should be used with considerable sensitivity to their underling limitations. Until a number of the identified problems can be resolved satisfactorily, a reasonable stance for the practitioner is to use assessment instruments judiciously, preferably in conjunction with other professionals for shared decision making and responsibility; to be aware that factors other than evidence influence the assessment process; and to call attention to the need for continuously updating, evaluating, and standardizing current assessment protocols.

INTERVENTION PROTOCOLS

Intervention protocols are less in evidence in the elder abuse literature relative to screening and assessment protocols. The dearth of intervention schemes may be the logical outcome of the inability to define elder maltreatment adequately or to identify the causes. If there is little clarity about the causes and the constitution of elder abuse, then it becomes doubly difficult to talk about effective intervention. The preoccupation with case detection, spurred on by the enactment of elder-abuse legislation, may also account for the stronger showing of assessment protocols in the literature. As well, there is the possibility that the ascendancy of the situational/caregiver stress model with its implied intervention of providing respite services made it unnecessary to document something so straightforward.

The goals of intervention are usually protection and prevention (Hudson and Johnson 1986), tempered by the reality that the legally competent adult has the right to determine what outcome of the intervention, if any, is acceptable. Practitioners have frequently voiced their feelings of helplessness when confronted with victims who have refused assistance (Bergman 1989); have expressed discomfort with the uneasy mixture of legal and therapeutic options open to them; and have repeatedly called attention to their concerns about protecting client's rights (Phillips 1989). Some of these problems can be alleviated if agencies or institutions have set procedures and time frames that can be followed when the practitioner encounters abuse. Protocols help to guide the practitioner through a number of pre-planned steps or options and anticipated problems that should help with the management of the consequences of maltreatment.

The available protocols represent a variety of approaches to intervention but usually contain legal, therapeutic, educational, environmental, and advocacy components (O'Malley et al. 1983; Astrein et al. 1984; Podnieks 1985; Ansello et al. 1986; Kinderknecht 1986; Quinn and Tomita 1986; Fulmer and O'Malley 1987; Breckman and Adelman 1989; Bergman 1989). Legal interventions involve the mobilization of the criminal-justice system for the protection of the elder and the possible prosecution of the abuser according to the laws of the state or the province as noted in Chapters 3 and 4. The therapeutic aspects tend to fall under the rubric of counselling, and represent a wide range of established therapies (e.g., cognitive therapy, psychotherapy, family systems therapy) to be used in conjunction with the principles of crisis intervention (immediate action to stabilize), short-term treatment (relief of symptoms), and long-term treatment ("cure"). Educational approaches generally include information about abuse and neglect, aging, caregiving, and self-protection, while environmental tactics involve the marshalling of core services and/or changing the living circumstances of the abused. Advocacy would be linking the caregiver and the victim to what is needed.

Some of the protocols list the options for intervention (Podnieks 1985; Quinn and Tomita 1986), some provide decision paths (Fulmer and O'Malley 1987), while others move the practitioner through a series of stages (Breckman and Adelman 1988; Bergman 1989). Many of the guiding frameworks or protocols identify a range of target groups beginning with the individual as client through to the community as client (Podnieks 1985; Quinn and Tomita 1986). All frameworks include the caregiver as a target for intervention. None appear to address the problems of abuse in the institution, although community education might serve this purpose. The intervention protocols usually do not stand alone but are accompanied by discussions about their use (Breckman and Adelman 1988). The guiding framework for intervention developed by Podnieks (1985) is provided as an example in Appendix C.

The apparent problems with the screening and the assessment protocols are carried through to intervention strategies. Three fundamental observations can be made about the intervention protocols: the assumptions of the situational/caregiver model are pervasive; indicators of what strategies should be used with whom under what circumstances are ill defined; the treatments are unproven.

Undoubtedly, caregiver stress is one of the factors involved in elder abuse and neglect, but there are enough dissimilar phenomena subsumed under abuse to warrant different approaches to intervention (Podnieks 1989). Several studies have revealed at least three distinct categories of abuse, each requiring a different type of intervention. At minimum, there is the impaired elder whose needs have been temporarily neglected because of a burdened caregiver; there is the impaired elder who is not dependent on the caregiver but who has been financially exploited and psychologically abused; and there are those elderly who are not dependent and have not been abused by caregivers but by other family members (O'Malley et al. 1984; Wolf et al. 1984). Only the first category is pertinent to the caregiver stress model, but every protocol directs the practitioner to provide education about caregiver stress and to mobilize the appropriate formal services. What to do with the mentally ill or the developmentally handicapped adult child or an abusive spouse or a set of formal caregivers in an institution is left to the practitioner's imagination.

Lurking beneath the surface of the caregiver stress model is the more insidious problem that goes beyond blaming the victim (Pillemer 1986) — the victim can be harmed. If any credence can be accorded to the previously mentioned study by Phillips and Rempusheski (1986), the practitioners were loathe to report abuse even when the client's life was in danger as long as the caregivers exhibited the appropriate behaviours (cooperating with the practitioner, having the best of intentions, etc.), and the reasons for their behaviour were understandable — the old person was "difficult," or the caregiver had a history of mental health problems or alcoholism, or was simply old! While there were other considerations involved, caregiver needs, as the target for intervention, took precedence over the needs of the victim. It is unknown if the practitioners in this study followed a protocol. However, the hold the caregiver hypothesis had on the respondents was clearly tenacious.

Not many of the guiding frameworks for intervention appear to provide indicators as to what to use, with whom, and under what circumstances according to (1) the content of the intervention (empowerment, consciousness building, managing depression); (2) the process (educational vs. therapeutic vs. environmental vs. advocacy); or (3) the modality (individual, couple, family, or group). One study based on practitioners' responses to elder abuse vignettes found that the interventions chosen varied according to the perceived severity of the abuse, the occupation of the professional, and the relationship of the victim to the abuser (Pratt et al. 1983). While this study implied some match between the problem and the intervention, Phillips and Rempusheski (1986) discovered that the match between the diagnosis and the intervention in their investigation was surprisingly poor. As an illustration, the practitioner would choose a self-protective intervention (e.g., closing a case) when abuse was clearly diagnosed. And the strength of the intervention (for example, the use of education) did not fit with the diagnosis when stronger measures were indicated. Most current intervention protocols, except perhaps the intervention process laid out by Fulmer and O'Malley (1987), would do little to correct for these inadequate choices.

An important reason why intervention strategies are not more precise probably reflects the lack of studies evaluating the relative effectiveness of different interventions or of any intervention (Hudson and Johnson 1986). In the earlier investigations of elder abuse (Block and Sinnott 1979; O'Malley et al. 1979; McLaughlin et al. 1980; Chen et al. 1981; Wolf et al. 1982), between 36 percent and 70 percent of the cases were reportedly not resolved satisfactorily. It was not known what constituted resolution, or to whose satisfaction, and it was not clear what interventions were considered. Certainly, clinical reports describe what has been found to be effective in working with older abused persons (cf. Quinn and Tomita 1986; Fulmer and O'Malley 1987; Ringel Segal and Iris 1989), but these findings have been mainly impressionistic. In brief, the intervention strategies suggested in most protocols have not been evaluated in terms of outcomes, nor has the comparative effectiveness of the interventions been tested. At the very least, the relationship between interventions designed to reduce caregiver stress and the cessation of abuse should receive empirical confirmation.

The problems with intervention protocols are variations on the same theme found in the discussions of screening and assessment protocols and need not be repeated. The perplexing question is why practitioners continue to embrace the caregiver stress model as the mainstay of intervention when there are other identified causes of elder abuse. Some authors have speculated that the appeal of the caregiver stress model lies in its provision of immediate answers to overwhelming problems (Phillips 1983), buttressed by the burgeoning gerontological research in Canada and the United States that portrays the families of older persons as willing, responsible caregivers (Pillemer 1986). It would seem that the skills used in working with other elderly client populations are being transferred to the elder abuse field without much consideration as to their appropriateness. At the same time, research of Pillemer and his associates about the perils of spouse abuse seems to go unheeded, possibly because the dynamics of spouse abuse and its treatment are unfamiliar to gerontological practitioners.

CONCLUSIONS

In this chapter, we have reviewed the available screening, assessment, and intervention protocols that guide professional practice. Given the existence of these protocols, one could easily be led to believe that there is extensive knowledge about the cause, consequences, and management of elder abuse. However, a review of the major protocols acutely shows how the confusion in theory and the disarray in the research has spilled over into practice, where situations are very complicated and the stakes are regrettably higher. All of the tools developed to help the practitioner suffer from inadequate definitions of abuse and neglect, which in turn are not adequately distinguished; there is a bias in favour of caregiver stress from screening through to intervention; there is an overreliance on judgement under the guise of objectivity; and there has been little field testing of the tools to unscramble some of the more pressing problems that are amenable to change. An awareness of these issues suggests that a cautious stance is needed on the part of the practitioner when called upon to use these protocols. These issues also clearly point to the need for a willingness to evaluate the wisdom of existing protocols as new conceptualizations lead to different interpretations of maltreatment.

CHAPTER 7

ELDER ABUSE AND NEGLECT: FUTURE CONSIDERATIONS

In this monograph, we have provided an overview of elder abuse and neglect from a number of different perspectives. By now, it should be obvious that the knowledge of elder mistreatment is severely limited, despite the voluminous literature devoted to the topic. Not only is there a shortage of reliable information, but what is taken to be fact is suspect by virtue of being predicated on poorly designed research. At the same time, there seems to be a reluctance to search for or accept new informa-tion as it becomes available. And the oft repeated refrain — there is a pau-city of Canadian research — is especially apt in the case of elder abuse and neglect.

Because of the impreciseness in our definitions of elder abuse and neglect and the differences between the two concepts, we do not know the extent of these problems. An inability to identify the social parameters of abuse and neglect has not prevented Canadians from developing poli-cies that are encased in the legislation of several provinces. The vague definitions of elder mistreatment and the influence of the child welfare model on the legislation have, in turn, generated a host of controversies. Most notably, the lack of due process safeguards in some of the legisla-tion has been flagged for serious attention. Thus, to protect the liberty and the autonomy of Canada's seniors, there is a need for clearly defined criteria for intervention. Yet, when screening, assessment, and interven-tion protocols are closely examined, we have more of the same — defini-tional confusion, judgement masquerading as objectivity, and no empirical confirmation of what constitutes an effective service or intervention.

These problems are not insurmountable, and in fact we would argue that Canada is in a unique position by virtue of the fact that the nation has not been committed to one course of action in tackling the problems of elder abuse and neglect. What is more, we are considered "behind" in the development of legislation compared to the United States (Hooy-man 1989). This could be considered a distinct advantage. There are still many options available that can be considered in the light of the experiences in the United States and in the Atlantic provinces. These options should take into account Canadian and American differences, especially in the areas of health and social services delivery systems.

In this chapter, we conclude with a consideration of the policy options that seem most compelling, given our review of the elder mistreatment literature. Our final comments are directed at immediate research needs. Research needs are discussed after policy issues because the case of elder mistreatment policy has jumped ahead of the research and appears to be the most pressing concern.

SOCIAL POLICY

The Legislative Approach

If protective legislation is developed, a number of important issues would have to be carefully considered. The experience in the United States and in the Atlantic provinces shows that, all too often, this type of legislation is seriously flawed, embodying criteria that are vague and discriminatory, and failing to achieve an acceptable balance between paternalism and respect for autonomy. Particular attention would have to be focused on the following issues:

1) The least restrictive alternative should be employed in order to protect the elderly from abuse without unduly infringing on their privacy and personal freedom (Horstman 1975; Harewood 1981; Note 1983; Sharpe 1983, 1988; Sloan 1983; Gordon et al. 1986; Metcalf 1986; Hughes 1988). For example, the legislation in several American jurisdictions, including Arkansas, Florida, Idaho, Massachusetts, Kentucky, and the District of Columbia, expressly provides that, in deciding what type of protective order to issue, the court must choose the one that is the least restrictive of personal liberty and most conducive to promoting maximum self-determination (Sloan 1983; Lee 1986; Lewis 1986; Metcalf 1986). A similar provision is contained in the new legislation in Prince Edward Island. In Canada, the adoption of this philosophy is essential in view of the *Canadian Charter of Rights and Freedoms* (1982).

2) If protection legislation is developed, it should be based on proven vulnerability and need rather than on age. Age-based intervention both reflects and promotes discrimination, and might well contravene section 15(1) of the *Canadian Charter of Rights and Freedoms*.

3) The criteria for intervention, including terminology such as "abuse" and "in need of protection," must be defined with as much precision as possible. This is the one aspect of the Atlantic legislation that has been most frequently criticized. Consideration

might also be given to restricting the powers of intervention to cases of serious (and perhaps even repeated) abuse, as in the Prince Edward Island Act and some of the most recent U.S. legislation.

4) The integrity and the autonomy of the family unit should be respected, unless this is inconsistent with providing the needed protection (Sharpe 1988).

5) Primary emphasis should be placed on the provision of voluntary support services within the community (Harewood 1981; Faulkner 1982; Kapp 1983; Note 1983; Bissett-Johnson 1986; Quinn and Tomita 1986; Sharpe 1987, 1988). Involuntary intervention and removal, even for a short term, should only be adopted as a last resort (Faulkner 1982; Krauskopf and Burnett 1983).

6) Intervention legislation must make adequate provision for due process protection. Intervention constitutes a serious encroachment on personal liberty and autonomy, and it is therefore essential, particularly in view of the *Canadian Charter of Rights and Freedoms* (1982) that proper safeguards be implemented. As Metcalf notes:

> Care must be taken that in our zeal to protect the elderly, we do not rob them of their fundamental rights. Protection at the expense of dignity may harm the elderly more than abuse or self-neglect. [1986, 777].

Non-Legislative Approach: Advocacy

Given the limitations of, and the complex issues associated with, legislative responses to the problem of elder abuse, it could be useful to consider a non-legislative approach — specifically, the use of an adult advocate. This approach assumes that the least intrusive mechanisms could be used to assist elderly victims of abuse, neglect, and exploitation. The advocate's major functions would be to assist the victim in gaining access to community services. The advocate would inform clients of their rights and of the alternatives to services. Some of the key characteristics of the advocacy approach are summarized below.

1) The advocacy approach should be guided by clearly defined objectives and goals and have dedicated resources for responding to clients' needs.

2) The formal component of the advocacy approach should be independent from the service delivery, case management system.

3) The advocacy approach should provide assistance to individual vulnerable adults for protecting their rights and meeting their needs. In addition, this approach could lobby social and political

systems to bring about systemic changes to benefit vulnerable adults in general.

4) Since the goal of the advocacy approach should be to intrude as little as possible, the program would not need legislated powers of intervention. However, certain regulated powers of investigation may be necessary. These powers would be consistent with maintaining the rights of the elderly to privacy and would not pose a threat to their personal freedom. Powers of intervention, such as rights of entry and the provision of services without the consent of the elderly person, should not be part of advocacy. In cases of emergency, power of entry could be provided through another legislative power.

SERVICES

The few studies evaluating services for the neglected and abused elderly are not clear as to what is effective in combating mistreatment. What is clear, however, is as follows:

1) New or unique services are not necessarily required in response to elder abuse, since the services already available for old persons provide the necessary resources used in response to elder abuse.

2) Home care and emergency housing services are in short supply in the United States. In Canada, most provinces have home care and home-maker services, although they vary in terms of what services are provided and in the quality of the coordination (Chappell et al. 1986; Forbes et al. 1987). Housing options (see Gutman and Blackie 1985) could be modified to serve the needs of the abused. In particular, respite care services (beds in long-term care institutions and day respite in the form of adult day care or day hospital) could be more evenly developed across Canada to provide emergency help for victims (see Chappell et al. 1986).

It would seem, then, that a reasonable option for service delivery would be the expansion, modification, and coordination of already existing health and social services for the elderly. This approach would ensure their ready accessibility rather than the establishment of a new set of services to deal specifically with elder mistreatment.

FUTURE RESEARCH

The review of the elder abuse literature would suggest that almost every issue requires the attention of researchers. However, research dollars are stretched and there are only a handful of Canadian scholars working in this area. The most immediate research should directly link policy to practice.

1) It is highly unlikely that Canadian researchers would ever agree on the definitions of abuse and neglect. However, a moratorium by the small number of researchers involved could be temporarily declared so that meaningful operational definitions for the major forms of maltreatment found in the literature (physical abuse, psychological abuse, and neglect) could be developed. Material abuse should be added to the list, since there are some indications that this is a problem for Canadians (Shell 1982; Podnieks et al. 1989). The definitions used by Podnieks et al. (1989) could serve as a starting point for these discussions. The definitions should be empirically tested in different sites across Canada, including within institutions.

2) A national prevalence survey of elder abuse and neglect has only recently been conducted in Canada (Podnieks et al. 1989). Serious consideration should be given to including some of the same questions about elder mistreatment in other national surveys in the future in order to monitor the extent of the problem. This type of information would provide rough indicators about whether or not the problem is growing.

3) Legislative initiatives in the Atlantic provinces, and those pertaining to institutions, should be seriously evaluated according to the purposes they were designed to achieve.

4) If about 4 percent of older Canadians reportedly suffer maltreatment (Podnieks et al. 1989), researchers should begin to study the implications this figure has for the demand of services and the manpower required to solve the problem.

5) Practitioners are in a very difficult position, given the weaknesses identified in screening and assessment. Research should be conducted to refine the available screening and assessment instruments, with a particular emphasis on the antecedents and consequences of abuse.

6) Existing intervention programs need to be evaluated to ascertain their effects on the persons involved and their contribution to solving the problems of elder mistreatment.

7) The nature and the extent of abuse and neglect in Canadian institutions have never been systematically investigated. Speculation and opinion must be set aside and replaced with factual data before we forge ahead to change policies and practices.

8) The development of different theories to explain the different forms of elder abuse and neglect will ultimately put an end to

the definitional dilemmas. Canadian scholars in the fields of family violence and gerontology would do well to think and work together on collaborative projects.

The list of research suggestions could go on indefinitely. However, in Canada it is evident that we must get down to the "basics" as the first priority of research.

CONCLUSIONS

In this monograph we have used a critical perspective regarding the theories, research, policy, and practices pertaining to elder abuse and neglect. Policy, programs, and practice are being erected on an insufficient theoretical and research foundation that may have serious repercussions for our older citizens.

Although it has become almost fashionable to critique the definitions of abuse and neglect, this process is extremely important for a number of reasons. The definitions find their way into the legislation, where they dictate certain action and where they direct the flow of resources. Some of these definitions have been found to be ageist in nature, and are in danger of violating the rights of older persons. Moreover, to construct whole new service systems to categorically deal with elder mistreatment may "rob" other senior programs of vital resources (Callahan 1988). In the absence of clear definitions, it is difficult to know the incidence and the prevalence of the problem. Inadequate information leaves the door open for the media or professional groups to magnify the problem, to perpetuate stereotypes (granny bashing), and to underestimate the seriousness of the problem. While the magnitude of the suffering should not be the basis for capturing the attention of the public or of politicians (and, hence, capturing dollars), the knowlege of the parameters of the problem could avoid generating unreasonable fears among the elderly and promote realistic responses to the problem.

Weak theoretical explanations of elder mistreatment or the unwillingness to recognize that there may be many different explanations brings premature closure to solutions and enhances the possibility of employing inappropriate, and perhaps dangerous, solutions. The caregiver stress model, although appropriate in some situations, is at risk of blaming the victim. If older persons are vulnerable because of the dependency of other family members, not because of their own dependency, then policies, programs, and interventions pertaining to the Canadian family might be in order.

Creative and well-designed research will not put an end to these problems until definitional and theoretical issues are addressed. In the meantime, it is alarming that inadequate existing research has become accepted as "fact." We conclude that few "facts" exist, and therefore practitioners must guard against applying myths to clinical practice, since possible harm might be the outcome.

None of these observations should be misconstrued as suggesting that Canadians need not be concerned about elder mistreatment. Assuring that older Canadians have the right to live in a safe environment and that their freedom in old age is unfettered is a serious social and legal matter — so serious that we believe that the identified issues need to be discussed soon and carefully, preferably in conjunction with older persons, before we forge ahead and develop more inappropriate policies, programs, and services.

APPENDIX A

High Risk Placement Worksheet

Name of Client/Patient: _____

A. Characteristics of Older Person   Existence of Risks
  1. Female   _____
  2. Advanced Age   _____
  3. Dependent   _____
  4. Problem Drinker   _____
  5. Intergenerational Conflict _____
  6. Internalizer   _____
  7. Excessive Loyalty   _____
  8. Past Abuse   _____
  9. Stoicism   _____
 10. Isolation   _____
 11. Impairment   _____
 12. Provocative Behavior   _____

B. Characteristics of Caregiver   Existence of Risks
  1. Problem Drinker   _____
  2. Medication/Drug Abuser   _____
  3. Senile Dementia/Confusion   _____
  4. Mental/Emotional Illness   _____
  5. Caregiving Inexperience   _____
  6. Economically Troubled   _____
  7. Abused as a Child   _____
  8. Stressed   _____
  9. Unengaged Outside the Home _____
 10. Blamer   _____
 11. Unsympathetic   _____
 12. Lacks Understanding   _____
 13. Unrealistic Expectations   _____
 14. Economically Dependent   _____
 15. Hypercritical   _____

C. Characteristics of Family System   Existence of Risks
   1. Lack of Family Support   _____
   2. Caregiving Reluctance   _____
   3. Overcrowding   _____
   4. Isolation   _____
   5. Marital Conflict   _____
   6. Economic Pressures   _____
   7. Intra-Family Problems   _____
   8. Desire for Institutionalization   _____
   9. Disharmony in Shared Responsibility   _____

D. Congruity of Perceptions Between Older   Existence of Risks
   Person and (Potential) Caregiver
   1. Quality of Past Relationship   _____
     a. Perception of Older Person _____
     b. Perception of Caregiver   _____
   2. Quality of Present Relationship   _____
     a. Perception of Older Person _____
     b. Perception of Caregiver   _____
   3. Referred Placement Location   _____
     a. Perception of Older Person _____
     b. Perception of Caregiver   _____
   4. Ideal Placement Location   _____
     a. Perception of Older Person _____
     b. Perception of Caregiver   _____

SOURCE: J.I. Kosberg, "Preventing Elder Abuse: Identification of High Risk Factors Prior to Placement Decisions," *The Gerontologist* 28 (1988):48. Reproduced with permission.

APPENDIX B

Data Collection Tool for Assessment of
Possible Elder Neglect and/or Abuse

ASSESSMENT OF CLIENT

A. *Indicators of possible neglect*
   1. General appearance:
      a) clothing: b) hygiene: c) grooming:
         disarrayed _____   body odor _____   unkept hair __
         torn _____   unclean _____   uncut nails ____
         soiled _____   unshaven _____
         worn _____
   2. Nutritional status: pallor _____   dry lips _____
                            sunken
                            eyes/cheeks_____
   3. Time spent alone: always _____   usually_____
                            rarely _____   never _____
   4. Assistance needed with: If needed, how often received?
                      no   yes   usually   rarely   never
      a) bathing _____
      b) dressing _____
      c) eating _____
      d) medication _____
      e) mobility_____
      f) toileting_____
      g) finances_____
   5. Satisfaction with assistance received:
         usually _____ rarely _____ never _____

B. *Physical indicators of possible abuse*
   1. Observe for presence of: client's
                                location   description   explanation
      a) abrasions _____
      b) alopecia _____
      c) bruises_____

107

    d) burns _____

    e) decubitus ulcers _____

    f) fractures _____

    g) lacerations _____

    h) limited ROM _____

    i) pain/tenderness _____

    j) physical disability_____

    k) welts _____

2. Behaviour toward caregiver during encounter:

    lack of physical contact _____

    lack of facial contact _____

    lack of eye contact_____

    lack of verbal contact _____

C. *Cognitive emotional indicators of possible abuse*

    1. Orientation:

	oriented	disoriented
a) orientation to person		
b) orientation to place		
c) orientation to time		

    2. Speech:

        a) amount: talkative _____ taciturn _____ silent _____

        b) clarity: mumbling ____ slurred _____

        c) rate: fast _____ hesitant _____ slow_____

        d) volume: loud_____ soft _____ inaudible ____

    3. Mood/affect:

        apathetic_____   anxious _____

        depressed _____   fearful_____

        sad _____

    4. Attitude toward nurse during encounter:

        defensive _____   evasive _____

        guarded _____   hostile_____

        irritable _____   suspicious _____

    5. Attitude toward caregiver during encounter:

        defensive _____   guarded _____

        hostile_____   passive _____

ASSESSMENT OF CAREGIVER

1. Relationship to client: relative: _____ other: _____

2. Age: 21-39 _____   3. Sex: female _____

       40-59 _____   male _____

       60+ _____

4. Marital Status:
    married _____
    single _____
    separated _____
    divorced _____

5. Living arrangements:
    alone _____
    with client _____
    with spouse _____
    with children _____
    with others _____

6. Source of income:
    UIC _____
    employment _____
    other _____
    welfare _____
    family _____

7. History of:
    alcohol abuse _____
    drug abuse _____
    family violence _____
    physical illness _____
    mental illness _____
    mental retardation _____

8. Sources of stress:
    financial _____
    fatigue _____
    lack of space _____
    lack of leisure time _____
    marital discord _____
    problems with children _____
    lifestyle disrupted due to caregiving role _____

9. Knowledge of client's situation: excellent   good   poor
    a) physical/emotional health _____
    b) needed assistance with ADL:
        bathing _____
        dressing _____
        eating _____
        mobility _____
        toileting _____
    c) medical treatment regime:
        medication _____
        diet _____
        rest _____
        exercise _____
        treatments _____

10. Attitude toward client during encounter:
    angry _____
    blaming _____
    critical _____
    overconcerned _____
    resentful _____
    underconcerned _____

11. Attitude toward nurse during encounter:
    defensive _____
    guarded _____
    evasive _____
    hostile _____
    irritable _____
    suspicious _____

Appendix B

12. Behavior with client during encounter:
      lack of physical contact _____
      lack of facial contact _____
      lack of eye contact _____
      lack of verbal contact _____

SOURCE: M.M. Ross, P.A. Ross, and M. Ross-Carson, "Abuse of the Elderly," *The Canadian Nurse* 81 (1985):38. Reprinted with permission.

APPENDIX C

Intervention

PRIMARY PREVENTION

Research: To determine the causes leading to abuse
             To develop a valid and reliable assessment tool
Education: To increase public and professional awareness of the abuse
             problem
             To further understanding of the aging process

SECONDARY PREVENTION

- Establishment of screening programs for elder abuse
- Medical intervention for treatment of injuries; treatment of abuser
- Develop plan of intervention to address elder abuse
- Provision of protective services/legal intervention/guardianship
- Coordination of community support system to ensure quality continuum care. Stress reducing measures through informal supports, networking, peer counselling and appropriate formal services
- Family therapy involving elder, abuser, other family members
- Educational programs to teach effective caretaking roles using a problem-solving process

TERTIARY PREVENTION

- Rehabilitation, assisting the elder to achieve his/her optimum level of health and safety, may involve permanent change to create a more supportive environment
- Rehabilitation of abuser — ongoing counselling, group support

SOURCE: E. Podnieks, "Elder Abuse: It's Time We Did Something About It," *The Canadian Nurse* 81 (December 1985):39. Reprinted with permission.

BIBLIOGRAPHY

Advocacy Centre for the Elderly
  1988   *Elder Abuse — The Hidden Crime*. Toronto.
Alberta Civil Liberties Research Centre
  1988   *Do Not Go Gently: Law, Liberty and Aging in Alberta*. Calgary, Alta.
Alberta Law Reform Institute
  1990   *Report for Discussion on Enduring Powers of Attorney*. Edmonton, Alta.
Alberta Senior Citizens Secretariat
  1987   *Elder Abuse and Neglect*.
Alliance/Elder Abuse Project
  1983   *An Analysis of States' Mandatory Reporting Laws on Elder Abuse*. Syracuse, N.Y.: Catholic Charities.
Anderson, T.B.
  1989   "Community Professionals and Their Perspectives on Elder Abuse." Pp. 117-26 in R. Filinson and S.R. Ingman (eds.), *Elder Abuse: Practice and Policy*. New York: Human Sciences Press.
Anetzberger, G.J.
  1989   "Implications of Research on Elder Abuse Perpetrators: Rethinking Current Social Policy and Programming." Pp. 43-50 in R. Filinson and S.R. Ingman (eds.), *Elder Abuse: Practice and Policy*. New York: Human Sciences Press.
Ansello, E.F., N.R. King, and G. Taler
  1986   "The Environmental Press Model: A Theoretical Framework for Intervention in Elder Abuse." Pp. 315-30 in K.A. Pillemer and R.S. Wolf (eds.), *Elder Abuse: Conflict in the Family*. Dover, Mass.: Auburn House Publishing Co.
Astrein, B., A. Steinberg, and J. Duhl
  1984   *Working with Abused Elders: Assessment, Advocacy and Intervention*. Worcester, Mass.: University Center on Aging, University of Massachusetts, Medical Center.
Atkinson, S., M.F. Madill, D. Solberg, and T. Turner
  1985   "Mental Health Advocacy: Paradigm or Panacea?" *Canada's Mental Health* 33(3): 3–7.
Australian Law Reform Commission
  1987   *Community Law Reform for the Australian Capital Territory: Enduring Powers of Attorney*. Canberra: Australian Government Publishing Services.

Beattie, W.M.
  1976   "Aging and the Social Services." Pp. 619-42 in R. Binstock and E.
          Shanas (eds.), *Handbook of Aging and the Social Services*. New York:
          Van Nostrand Reinhold.

Beaudry, M.
  1985   *Battered Women*. Montreal: Black Rose Books.

Bergman, J.A.
  1989   "Responding to Abuse and Neglect Cases: Protective Services versus
          Crisis Intervention." Pp. 94-103 in R. Filinson and S.R. Ingman
          (eds.), *Elder Abuse: Practice and Policy*. New York: Human Sciences
          Press.

Bissett-Johnson, A.
  1986   "Domestic Violence: A Plethora of Problems and Precious Few Solu-
          tions." *Canadian Journal of Family Law* 5:253-76.

Blake, B.
  1983   "Public Health and Guardianship: The Recluse." *Health Law in
          Canada* 4:10-13.

Blenkner, M., M. Bloom, M. Nielsen, and R. Weber
  1974   *Final Report: Protective Services for Older People: Findings from the Ben-
          jamin Rose Institute (Part 1)*. Cleveland, Ohio: Benjamin Rose Institute.

Block, M.R.
  1983   "Special Problems and Vulnerability of Elderly Women." Pp. 220-33
          in J.I. Kosberg (ed.), *Abuse and Maltreatment of the Elderly: Causes and
          Interventions*. Boston: John Wright-PSG.

Block, M.R., and J.D. Sinnott
  1979   *The Battered Elder Syndrome: An Exploratory Study*. Unpublished manu-
          script, Center for Aging, University of Maryland, College Park, Md.

Bookin, D., and R.E. Dunkle
  1985   "Elder Abuse: Issues for the Practitioner." *Social Casework* 66:3-12.

Borovoy, A.
  1982   "Guardianship and Civil Liberties." *Health Law in Canada* 3:51-57.

Boydston, L.S., and J.A. McNairn
  1981   "Elder Abuse by Adult Caretakers: An Exploratory Study." Pp.
          135-36 in *Physical and Financial Abuse of the Elderly* (Publication No.
          97-297). U.S. House of Representatives Select Committee on Aging.
          Washington, D.C.: U.S. Government Printing Office.

Breckman, R.S., and R.D. Adelman
  1988   *Strategies for Helping Victims of Elder Mistreatment*. Newbury Park,
          Calif.: Sage Publications.

Bristowe, E.
  1987   *Family Mediated Abuse of Non-Institutionalized Frail Elderly Men and
          Women Living in British Columbia*. Unpublished manuscript, Simon
          Fraser University, Gerontology Research Centre, Burnaby, B.C.

Bristowe, E., and J.B. Collins
  1989   "Family Mediated Abuse of Noninstitutionalized Frail Elderly Men
          and Women Living in British Columbia." *Journal of Elder Abuse and
          Neglect* 1(1): 45-64.

Cabness, J.
   1989   "The Emergency Shelter: A Model for Building the Self-Esteem of
            Abused Elders." *Journal of Elder Abuse and Neglect* 1(2): 71-89.
Caldwell, J.M., and M.B. Kapp
   1981   "The Rights of Nursing Home Patients: Possibilities and Limitations
            of Federal Regulation." *Journal of Health Politics, Policy and Law*
            6:40-48.
Callahan, J.J.
   1982   "Elder Abuse Programming: Will It Help the Elderly?" *The Urban
            and Social Change Review* 15:15-16.
   1988   "Elder Abuse: Some Questions for Policymakers." *The Gerontolo-
            gist* 28(4): 453-58.
Canadian Charter of Rights and Freedoms
   1982   Part I of the *Constitution Act,* 1982, Schedule B of the *Canada Act* 1982,
            Statutes of Canada 1980-81-82, c. 11 as amended.
Chance, P.
   1987   "Attacking Elderly Abuse." *Psychology Today* 21(9): 24-25.
Chappell, N.L., L.A. Strain, and A.A. Blandford
   1986   *Aging and Health Care: A Social Perspective.* Holt, Rinehart and Winston
            of Canada.
Chen, P.N., S. Bell, D. Dolinsky, J. Doyle, and M. Dunn
   1981   "Elderly Abuse in Domestic Settings: A Pilot Study." *Journal of
            Gerontological Social Work* 4(1): 3-17.
Christie, J.
   1982   "Guardianship: The Alberta Experience: A Model for Change."
            Health Law in Canada 3:58-66.
   1984   "Guardianship in Alberta, Canada." Pp. 183-226 in T. Apolloni and
            T.P. Cooke (eds.), *A New Look at Guardianship.* Baltimore, Md.: Paul
            H. Brookes Publishing.
Committee on Long Term Care for Senior Citizens
   1988   *A New Vision for Long Term Care: Meeting the Need.* Edmonton, Alta.:
            Government of Alberta.
Connidis, I.A.
   1989   *Family Ties and Aging.* Toronto: Butterworths.
Corin, E.
   1987   "The Relationship between Formal and Informal Social Support Net-
            works in Rural and Urban Contexts." Pp. 367-94 in V.W. Marshall
            (ed.), *Aging in Canada: Social Perspectives* (2d ed.). Markham, Ont.:
            Fitzhenry and Whiteside.
Council on Aging of Ottawa-Carleton
   1987   *Elder Abuse: Report of a Survey Conducted by the Ad Hoc Committee on
            Elder Abuse of the Council on Aging of Ottawa-Carleton.* February.
   1988   *Enhancing Awareness of Elder Abuse: Three Educational Models.*
Coward, R.T.
   1979   "Planning Community Services for the Rural Elderly: Implications
            for Research." *The Gerontologist* 19:275-82.

Crouse, J.S., D.C. Cobb, B.B. Harris, F.J. Kopecky, and J. Poertner
  1981   Abuse and Neglect of the Elderly in Illinois: Incidence and Characteristics,
          Legislation and Policy Recommendations. Unpublished manuscript.
          Springfield, Ill.: Sangamon State University and Illinois Department
          of Aging.

Crystal, S.
  1986   "Social Policy and Elder Abuse." Pp. 331-40 in K.A. Pillemer and
          R.S. Wolf (eds.), Elder Abuse: Conflict in the Family. Dover, Mass.:
          Auburn House Publishing Co.

  1987   "Elder Abuse: The Latest 'Crisis.' " Public Interest 88:56-66.

Davies, C.
  1984   Family Law in Canada. Toronto: Carswell Company.

Devitt, M., and B. Checkoway
  1982   "Participation in Nursing Home Resident Councils: Promise and
          Practice." The Gerontologist 22:49-53.

Douglas, D.S., D. Feinberg, R. Jacobsohn, and A.B. Stock
  1985   "Rx for the Elderly: Legal Rights (and Wrongs) within the Health
          Care System." Harvard Civil Rights-Civil Liberties Law Review
          20:425-83.

Douglass, R.L.
  1983   "Domestic Neglect and Abuse of the Elderly: Implications for
          Research and Service." Family Relations 32:395-402.

Douglass, R.L., and T. Hickey
  1983   "Domestic Neglect and Abuse of the Elderly: Research Findings and
          a Systems Perspective for Social Service Delivery Planning."
          Pp. 115-33 in J.I. Kosberg (ed.), Abuse and Maltreatment of the Elderly:
          Causes and Interventions. Boston: John Wright-PSG.

Douglass, R.L., T. Hickey, and C. Noel
  1980   A Study of Maltreatment of the Elderly and Other Vulnerable Adults. Final
          Report to U.S. Administration on Aging and the Michigan State
          Department of Social Services, Ann Arbor.

Dowd, J.
  1980   Stratification among the Aged. Monterey, Calif.: Brooks/Cole Publish-
          ing Co.

Dunkle, R.E., S.W. Poulshock, B. Silverstone, and G.T. Deimling
  1983   "Protective Services Reanalyzed: Does Casework Help or Harm?"
          Social Casework 64:195-99.

Endicott, T.A.O.
  1987   "The Criminality of Wife Assault." University of Toronto Faculty of
          Law Review 45:355-93.

Estes, C.L.
  1979   The Aging Enterprise. San Francisco: Jossey-Bass.

Estes, C.L., J. Swan, and L. Gerard
  1982   "Dominant and Competing Paradigms in Gerontology: Towards a
          Political Economy of Aging." Aging and Society 2:151-64.

Falcioni, D.
  1982   "Assessing the Abused Elderly." *Journal of Gerontological Nursing* 8(4): 208-12.
Faulkner, L.R.
  1982   "Mandating the Reporting of Suspected Cases of Elder Abuse: An Inappropriate, Ineffective and Ageist Response to the Abuse of Older Adults." *Family Law Quarterly* 16:69-91.
Ferguson, D., and C. Beck
  1983   "H.A.L.F. — Tool to Assess Elder Abuse within the Family." *Geriatric Nursing* 4:301-4.
Finkelhor, D., and K. Pillemer
  1984   "Elder Abuse: Its Relationship to Other Forms of Domestic Violence." Paper presented at the Second National Conference on Family Violence Research, Durham, New Hampshire.
Filinson, R.
  1989   "Introduction." Pp. 17-34 in R. Filinson and S.R. Ingman (eds.), *Elder Abuse: Practice and Policy.* New York: Human Sciences Press.
Foot, D.K.
  1982   *Canada's Population Outlook: Demographic Futures and Economic Challenges.* Toronto: James Lorimer.
Forbes, W.F., J.A. Jackson, and A.S. Kraus
  1987   *Institutionalization of the Elderly in Canada.* Toronto: Butterworths.
Fram Committee. *See* Ontario Advisory Committee on Substitute Decision Making for Mentally Incapable Persons 1987.
Fridman, G.H.
  1986   *The Law of Contract in Canada.* Toronto: Carswell Company.
Fulmer, T.
  1982   "Elder Abuse Detection and Reporting." *Massachusetts Nurse* (May):10-12.
  1989   "Clinical Assessment of Elder Abuse." Pp. 77-85 in R. Filinson and S.R. Ingman (eds.), *Elder Abuse: Practice and Policy.* New York: Human Sciences Press.
Fulmer, T., and V.M. Cahill
  1984   "Assessing Elder Abuse: A Study." *Journal of Gerontological Nursing* 10(12): 16-20.
Fulmer, T., and T.A. O'Malley
  1987   *Inadequate Care of the Elderly: A Health Care Perspective on Abuse and Neglect.* New York: Springer Publishing Co.
Gee, E., and M. Kimball
  1987   *Women and Aging.* Toronto: Butterworths.
Gelles, R.J.
  1979   *Family Violence.* Beverly Hills, Calif.: Sage Publications.
Ghent, W.R., N.P. Da Silva, and M.E. Farren
  1985   "Family Violence: Guidelines for Recognition and Management." *Canadian Medical Association Journal* 132: 541-53.
Gioglio, G.R., and P. Blakemore
  1983   *Elder Abuse in New Jersey: The Knowledge and Experience of Abuse among*

Older New Jerseyans. Unpublished manuscript, Department of Human Services, Trenton, N.J.

Giordano, N.H.
1982 *Individual and Family Correlates of Elder Abuse.* Ph.D. dissertation, University of Georgia.

Giordano, N.H., and J.A. Giordano
1984 "Elder Abuse: A Review of the Literature." *Social Work* 29(3): 232-36.

Girard, P.
1988 "Elder Abuse and Its Impact on Hospital Social Work." Pp. 43-56 in B. Schlesinger and R. Schlesinger (eds.), *Abuse of the Elderly: Issues and Annotated Bibliography.* Toronto: University of Toronto Press.

Godkin, M.A., R.S. Wolf, and K.A. Pillemer
1989 "A Case-Comparison Analysis of Elder Abuse and Neglect." *International Journal of Aging and Human Development* 28(3): 207-25.

Goldstein, S.E., and A. Blank
1988 "The Elderly: Abuse or Abusers?" Pp. 86-90 in B. Schlesinger and R. Schlesinger (eds.), *Abuse of the Elderly: Issues and Annotated Bibliography.* Toronto: University of Toronto Press.

Goldstein, V., G. Regnery, and E. Wellin
1981 "Caretaker Role Fatigue." *Nursing Outlook* 29(1): 24–30.

Gordon, R.M., and S.N. Verdun-Jones
1985 "Privatization and Protective Services for the Elderly: Some Observations on the Economics of the Aging Process." *International Journal of Law and Psychiatry* 8:311-25.

1987 "The Implications of the Canadian Charter of Rights and Freedoms for the Law Relating to Guardianship and Trusteeship." *International Journal of Law and Psychiatry* 10:21–34.

Gordon, R.M., S.N. Verdun-Jones, and D.J. MacDougall
1986 *Standing in Their Shoes: Guardianship, Trusteeship and the Elderly Canadian.* Burnaby, B.C.: Simon Fraser University, Criminology Research Centre.

1987 "Reforms in the Field of Adult Guardianship Law: A Comment on Recent Developments." *Canadian Journal of Family Law* 6:149-54.

Gottfredson, S.D., and D.M. Gottfredson
1988 "Violence Prediction Methods: Statistics and Clinical Strategies." *Violence and Victims* 3(4): 303-24.

Gourash, N.
1978 "Help-Seeking: A Review of the Literature." *American Journal of Community Psychology* 6:413-23.

Guillemard, A.M.
1980 *La vieillesse et l'état.* Paris: Presses Universitaires de France.

Guinn, M.J.
1985 "Elder Abuse and Neglect Raise New Dilemmas." *Generations* 10(2): 22-25.

Gutman, G., and N. Blackie (eds.)
1985 *Innovations in Housing and Living Arrangements for Seniors.* Burnaby, B.C.: Simon Fraser University, Gerontology Research Centre.

Hageboeck, J., and K. Brandt
1981   *Characteristics of Elderly Abuse.* Unpublished manuscript, Scott County, Iowa.

Hahn, P.H.
1976   *Crimes against the Elderly: A Study in Victimology.* Santa Cruz, Calif.: Davis Publishing Company.

Halamandaris, V.J.
1983   "Fraud and Abuse in Nursing Homes." Pp. 104-14 in J.I. Kosberg (ed.), *Abuse and Maltreatment of the Elderly: Causes and Interventions.* Boston: John Wright-PSG.

Hall, P.A., and S.R. Andrew
1984   *Minority Elder Maltreatment: Ethnicity, Gender, Age and Poverty.* Unpublished manuscript, San Antonio, Texas.

Hamilton, G.P.
1989   "Prevent Elder Abuse: Using a Family Systems Approach." *Journal of Gerontological Nursing* 15(3): 21-26.

Harewood, S.
1981   *Issues in Protective Services for Older Persons.* Unpublished manuscript, Senior Citizens Bureau, Alberta Social Services and Community Health.

Hayes, C.L., B. Soniat, and H. Burr
1986   "Value Conflict and Resolution in Forcing Services on 'At Risk' Community-Based Older Adults." *Clinical Gerontologist* 4(3): 41-48.

Hickey, T., and R.L. Douglass
1981   "Mistreatment of the Elderly in the Domestic Setting: An Exploratory Study." *American Journal of Public Health* 71(5): 500-7.

Hobbs, L.
1976   "Adult Protective Services: A New Program Approach." *Public Welfare* 34(3): 28-37.

Hooyman, N.
1983   "Elder Abuse and Neglect: Community Interventions." Pp. 376-90 in J.I. Kosberg (ed.), *Abuse and Mistreatment of the Elderly: Causes and Interventions.* Boston: John Wright-PSG.
1989   Review of B. Schlesinger and R. Schlesinger (eds.), *Abuse of the Elderly: Issues and Annotated Bibliography. Journal of Elder Abuse and Neglect* 1(2): 83-86.

Hornick, J., L. McDonald, G. Robertson, and J.E. Wallace
1988   *A Review of the Social and Legal Issues Concerning Family Abuse.* Calgary, Alta.: Canadian Research Institute for Law and the Family.

Horstman, P.M.
1975   "Protective Services for the Elderly: The Limits of Parens Patriae." *Missouri Law Review* 40:215-78.

Hudson, J.E.
1986   *Elder Abuse: An Overview.* Research Paper No. 7. Toronto: Programme in Gerontology, University of Toronto.

Hudson, M.F.
1986   "Elder Mistreatment: Current Research." Pp. 125-66 in K.A. Pillemer

and R.S. Wolf (eds.), *Elder Abuse: Conflict in the Family*. Dover, Mass.: Auburn House Publishing Co.

1989   "Analysis of the Concepts of Elder Mistreatment: Abuse and Neglect." *Journal of Elder Abuse and Neglect* 1(1): 5-25.

Hudson, M.F., and T.F. Johnson
1986   "Elder Neglect and Abuse: A Review of the Literature." *Annual Review of Gerontology and Geriatrics* 6:81-134.

Hughes, M.E.
1988   "Personal Guardianship and the Elderly in the Canadian Common Law Provinces: An Overview of the Law and Charter Implications." Pp. 138-56 in M.E. Hughes and E.D. Pask (eds.), *National Themes in Family Law*. Toronto: Carswell Company.

Hwalek, M.
1988   *Elder Abuse: The Illinois Department on Aging's Final Report on the Demonstration Program Act*. Unpublished manuscript prepared for the Illinois Department of Aging.

Johnson, S.H.
1985   "State Regulations of Long-Term Care: A Decade of Experience with Intermediate Sanctions." *Law, Medicine and Health Care* 13:173-87.

Jorgensen, B.
1986   *Crimes against the Elderly in Institutional Care*. Unpublished manuscript, Concerned Friends of Ontario Citizens in Care Facilities, Toronto, Ont.

Kammerman, S.B.
1976   "Community Services for the Aged: The View from Eight Countries." *The Gerontologist* 16:529-37.

Kane, R.L., and R.A. Kane
1985   *A Will and a Way: What the United States Can Learn from Canada about Caring for the Elderly*. New York: Columbia University Press.

Kapp, M.B.
1982   "Promoting the Legal Rights of Older Adults." *Journal of Legal Medicine* 3:367-412.

1983   "Adult Protective Services: Convincing the Patient to Consent." *Law, Medicine and Health Care* 11:163-67.

Katz, K.D.
1980   "Elder Abuse." *Journal of Family Law* 18:695-722.

Kinderknecht, C.H.
1986   "In Home Social Work with Abused or Neglected Elderly. An Experimental Guide to Assessment and Treatment." *Journal of Gerontological Social Work* (Spring): 29-42.

Kosberg, J.I.
1988   "Preventing Elder Abuse: Identification of High Risk Factors Prior to Placement Decisions." *The Gerontologist* 28(1): 43-50.

Krauskopf, J.M. and M.E. Burnett
1983   "The Elderly Person: When Protection Becomes Abuse." *Trial* 19:61-67.

Labarge, M.W.
    1988   "Elder Abuse: A Hidden Problem: How to Educate the Public."
            Paper presented at the 17th Annual Scientific and Educational Meet-
            ing of the Canadian Association on Gerontology, Halifax, Nova
            Scotia, October.

Lau, E. and J.I. Kosberg
    1979   "Abuse of the Elderly by Informal Care Providers." *Aging*
            (299-300):10-15.

Law Reform Commission of British Columbia
    1975   *Report on the Law of Agency, Part 2: Powers of Attorney and Mental Inca-*
            pacity. Vancouver, B.C.: Queen's Printer for British Columbia.

Law Reform Commission of Canada
    1984   *Working Paper on Assault.* Working Paper No. 38. Ottawa, Ont.: The
            Commission.

    1987   *Report on Recodifying the Criminal Law.* Report No. 31. Ottawa, Ont.:
            The Commission.

Law Reform Commission of Saskatchewan
    1981   *Tentative Proposals for a Guardianship Act, Part 1: Personal Guardian-*
            ship. Saskatoon, Sask.: L.R.C. of Saskatchewan.

    1983   *Proposals for a Guardianship Act, Part 1: Personal Guardianship.* Saska-
            toon, Sask.: L.R.C. of Saskatchewan.

Ledbetter Hancock, B.
    1990   *Social Work with Older People* (2d ed.) Englewood Cliffs, N.J.:
            Prentice-Hall.

Lee, D.
    1986   "Mandatory Reporting of Elder Abuse: A Cheap but Ineffective Solu-
            tion to the Problem." *Fordham Urban Law Journal* 14:723-71.

Lewis, L.A.
    1986   "Toward Eliminating the Abuse, Neglect, and Exploitation of
            Impaired Adults: The District of Columbia Adult Protective Services
            Act of 1984." *Catholic University Law Review* 35:1193-1213.

MacEachron, A.E., F.G. Bolton, R. Lanier, and W. Conley
    1985   *Elder Abuse: The Circle of Formal Violence.* Unpublished manuscript,
            Arizona State University, Tempe, Ariz.

MacLeod, L.
    1987   *Battered but Not Beaten. . . Preventing Wife Battering in Canada.* Cana-
            dian Advisory Council on the Status of Women, June.

Manitoba Law Reform Commission
    1974   *Report on Special, Enduring Powers of Attorney.* Winnipeg, Man.:
            Queen's Printer, Manitoba.

Manson, A.
    1987   *Advocacy in Psychiatric Hospitals: Evaluation of the Psychiatric Patient*
            Advocate Office. Report of the Evaluation Committee for the Psy-
            chiatric Patient Advocate Office. Toronto: Ontario Ministry of Health,
            Queen's Printer.

Marshall, V.
  1987　*Aging in Canada: Social Perspectives* (2nd ed.). Markham, Ont.: Fitz-
    henry and Whiteside.
Mastrocola-Morris, E.
  1989　*Woman Abuse: The Relationship between Wife Assault and Elder Abuse.*
    Prepared for the National Clearinghouse on Family Violence. Ottawa,
    Ont.: Minister of Supply and Services.
Matlow, J.R., and J.B. Mayer
  1986　"Elder Abuse: Ethical and Practical Dilemmas for Social Work."
    Health and Social Work 11:85-93.
McDaniel, S.A.
  1986　*Canada's Aging Population.* Toronto: Butterworths.
McDonald, P.L., W. Chisholm, T. Peressini, and T. Smillie
  1986　*A Review of a Second Stage Shelter for Battered Women and Children.*
    Ottawa, Ont.: National Welfare Directorate.
McLaughlin, C.
  1988　" 'Doing Good': A Worker's Perspective." *Public Welfare* 46(2): 29-32.
McLaughlin, J.S., J.P. Nickell, and L. Gill
  1980　"An Epidemiological Investigation of Elder Abuse in Southern Maine
    and New Hampshire." Pp. 111-47 in *Elder Abuse* (Publication No.
    68-463). U.S. House of Representatives Select Committee on Aging,
    Washington, D.C.: U.S. Government Printing Office, June 11.
McLaughlin, P.
  1979　*Guardianship of the Person.* Downsview, Ont.: National Institute on
    Mental Retardation.
McPherson, B.
  1990　*Aging as a Social Process: An Introduction to Individual and Population
    Aging* (2d ed.). Toronto: Butterworths.
Mercer, S.O.
  1983　"Consequences of Institutionalization of the Aged." Pp. 84-103 in
    J.I. Kosberg (ed.), *Abuse and Maltreatment of the Elderly: Causes and
    Interventions.* Boston: John Wright-PSG.
Metcalf, C.A.
  1986　"A Response to the Problem of Elder Abuse: Florida's Revised Adult
    Protections Act." *Florida State University Law Review* 14:745-77.
Mitchell, A.M.
  1979　"The Objects of Our Wisdom and Our Coercion: Involuntary
    Guardianship for Incompetents." *Southern California Law Review*
    52:1405-42.
Monk, A., and L.W. Kaye
  1982　"The Ombudsman Volunteer in the Nursing Home: Differential Role
    Perceptions of Patient Representatives for the Institutionalized
    Aged." *The Gerontologist* 22:194-99.
Montgomery, R.J.V., and E.F. Borgatta
  1986　"Possible Theories and the Development of Scientific Theory."
    Research on Aging 8(4): 586-608.

Moore, T., and V. Thompson
1987   "Elder Abuse: A Review of Research, Programmes, and Policy."
        The Social Worker 55(3): 115-22.
Moss, F.E., and V.J. Halamandaris
1977   *Too Old, Too Sick, Too Bad: Nursing Homes in America.* Germantown,
        Md.: Aspen Systems Corporation.
Nemore, P.
1985   "Protecting Nursing-Home Residents." *Trial* 21:54-61.
New Brunswick
1980   *Family Services Act,* Statutes of New Brunswick 1980, c. F-2.2 as
        amended.
New Brunswick Special Committee on Social Policy Development
1989   "Third Report." *Journal of the Legislative Assembly of New Brunswick,*
        May 19.
Newfoundland
1973   *Neglected Adults Welfare Act,* 1973, Statutes of Newfoundland 1973,
        c. 81, as amended.
Newfoundland Law Reform Commission
1988   *Enduring Powers of Attorney.* St. John's, Nfld.: N.L.R.C.
Note
1983   "Elder Abuse: The Merit of Mandatory Reporting Laws and the Min-
        nesota Response." *William Mitchell Law Review* 9:365-87.
Nova Scotia
1985   *Adult Protection Act,* Statutes of Nova Scotia 1985, c. 2, as amended.
Oakar, M.R., and C.A. Miller
1983   "Federal Legislation to Protect the Elderly." Pp. 422-35 in J.I. Kos-
        berg (ed.), *Abuse and Maltreatment of the Elderly: Causes and Interven-
        tions.* Boston: John Wright-PSG.
O'Brien, J.G., M.F. Hudson, and T.F. Johnson
1984   *Health Care Provider Survey on Elder Abuse.* Unpublished manuscript,
        East Lansing, Mich.
O'Malley, H., H. Segars, R. Perez, V. Mitchell, and G. Knuepfel
1979   *Elder Abuse in Massachusetts: A Survey of Professionals and Paraprofes-
        sionals.* Unpublished manuscript, Legal Research and Services for
        the Elderly, Boston, Mass.
O'Malley, T.A., D.E. Everitt , H.C. O'Malley, and W. Campion
1983   "Identifying and Preventing Family Mediated Abuse and Neglect
        of Elderly Persons." *Annals of Internal Medicine* 90(6): 998-1005.
O'Malley, T.A., H.C. O'Malley, D.E. Everitt, and D. Sarson
1984   "Categories of Family-Mediated Abuse and Neglect of Elderly Per-
        sons." *Journal of the American Geriatrics Society* 32:362-69.
Ontario Advisory Committee on Substitute Decision Making for Mentally
    Incapable Persons
1987   *Final Report.* Toronto.
Ontario Advisory Council on Senior Citizens
1986   *A Report on Elder Abuse.* Toronto.

Ontario Law Reform Commission
   1972   *Report on Powers of Attorney.* Toronto: Ministry of the Attorney
           General.

Ontario Ministry of the Attorney General
   1987   *You've Got a Friend: A Review of Advocacy in Ontario.* Report of the
           Review of Advocacy for Vulnerable Adults. Toronto: Queen's
           Printer. (O'Sullivan Review)

Opperman, D.S.
   1981   "Michigan's Bill of Rights for Nursing Home Residents." *Wayne Law
           Review* 27:1203-27.

O'Sullivan Review. *See* Ontario Ministry of the Attorney General 1987.

Palincsar, J., and D.C. Cobb
   1982   "The Physican's Role in Detecting and Reporting Elder Abuse." *Jour-
           nal of Legal Medicine* 3:413-41.

Pedrick-Cornell, C., and R.J. Gelles
   1982   "Elder Abuse: The Status of Current Knowledge." *Family Relations*
           31(3): 457-65.

Pennsylvania Department of Aging
   1982   *Elder Abuse in Pennsylvania.* Unpublished manuscript, Bureau of
           Advocacy, Harrisburg, Pa.

Pepper, C.D.
   1983   "Frauds against the Elderly." Pp. 68–83 in J.I. Kosberg (ed.), *Abuse
           and Maltreatment of the Elderly: Causes and Interventions.* Boston: John
           Wright-PSG.

Pepper, C.D., and M.R. Oaker
   1981   *Elder Abuse: An Examination of a Hidden Problem,* (Publication No.
           97-277). U.S. House of Representatives Select Committee on Aging.
           Washington, D.C.: U.S. Government Printing Office.

Phillips, L.R.
   1983   "Abuse and Neglect of the Frail Elderly at Home: An Exploration
           of Theoretical Relationships." *Journal of Advanced Nursing* 8(5): 379-92.

   1986   "Theoretical Explanations of Elder Abuse: Competing Hypotheses
           and Unresolved Issues." Pp. 197-217 in K.A. Pillemer and R.S. Wolf
           (eds.), *Elder Abuse: Conflict in the Family.* Dover, Mass.: Auburn House
           Publishing Co.

   1989   "Issues Involved in Identifying and Intervening in Elder Abuse."
           Pp. 86-93 in R. Filinson and S.R. Ingman (eds.), *Elder Abuse: Practice
           and Policy.* New York: Human Sciences Press.

Phillips, L.R., and V.F. Rempusheski
   1985   "A Decision-Making Model for Diagnosing and Intervening in Elder
           Abuse and Neglect." *Nursing Research* 34:134-39.

   1986   "Making Decisions about Elder Abuse." *Social Casework* 67(3): 131-40.
Phillips, N.M.
   1980   "Ohio's Bill of Rights for Nursing Home Patients." *University of Day-
           ton Law Review* 5:507-25.

Pillemer, K.A.
1985a   "The Dangers of Dependency: New Findings on Domestic Violence against the Elderly." *Social Problems* 33(2): 146-58.
1985b   *Domestic Violence against the Elderly.* Unpublished manuscript prepared for the Surgeon General's Workshop on Violence and Public Health, Leesberg, Virginia, October. Family Violence Research Program and Department of Sociology, Durham, N.H.
1986   "Risk Factors in Elder Abuse: Results from a Case-Control Study." Pp. 239-63 in K.A. Pillemer and R.S. Wolf (eds.), *Elder Abuse: Conflict in the Family.* Dover, Mass.: Auburn House Publishing Co.
1988   "Maltreatment of Patients in Nursing Homes: Overview and Research Agenda." *Journal of Health and Social Behavior* 29(3): 227-38.

Pillemer, K.A., and D. Finkelhor
1988   "The Prevalence of Elder Abuse: A Random Sample Survey." *The Gerontologist* 28(1): 51-57.
1989   "Causes of Elder Abuse: Caregiver Stress versus Problem Relatives." *American Journal of Orthopsychiatry* 59(2): 179-87.

Pillemer, K., and D.W. Moore
1989   "Abuse of Patients in Nursing Homes: Finding from a Survey of Staff." *The Gerontologist* 29(3): 314-20.

Pillemer, K., and J. Suitor
1988   "Elder Abuse." Pp. 247-70 in V.B. Van Hasselt, R.L. Morrison, A.S. Bellack, and M. Hensen (eds.), *Handbook of Family Violence.* New York: Plenum Press.

Podnieks, E.
1983   "Abuse of the Elderly." *The Canadian Nurse* 79(5): 34-35.
1985   "Elder Abuse: It's Time We Did Something about It." *The Canadian Nurse* 81(11): 36-39.
1988   "Elder Abuse: It's Time We Did Something about It." Pp. 32-42 in B. Schlesinger and R. Schlesinger (eds.), *Abuse of the Elderly: Issues and Annotated Bibliography.* Toronto: University of Toronto Press.
1989   *Abuse of the Elderly: When Caregivers Cease to Care.* Prepared for the National Clearinghouse on Family Violence. Ottawa, Ont.: Minister of Supply and Services.

Podnieks, E., K. Pillemer, J. Nicholson, J. Shillington, and A. Frizzell
1989   *National Survey on Abuse of the Elderly in Canada: Preliminary Findings.* Toronto: Office of Research and Innovation, Ryerson Polytechnical Institute.

Poertner, J.
1986   "Estimating the Incidence of Abused Older Persons." *Journal of Gerontological Social Work* 9(3): 3-15.

Poirier, D.
1988   "Models of Intervention for the Guardianship and Protection of Elderly Persons in Canada." Pp. 157-78 in M.E. Hughes and E.D. Pask (eds.), *National Themes in Family Law.* Toronto: Carswell Company.

Pratt, C.C., J. Koval, and S. Lloyd
  1983   "Service Workers' Responses to Abuse of the Elderly." *Social Case-
         work* 64:147-53.
Puttick, K.
  1985   "Enduring Powers of Attorney Act." *New Law Journal* 135:755-56.
Quinn, M.J., and S.K. Tomita
  1986   *Elder Abuse and Neglect: Causes, Diagnosis, and Intervention Strategies.*
         New York: Springer Publishing Co.
Rathbone-McCuan, E.
  1980   "Elderly Victims of Family Violence and Neglect." *Social Casework*
         61(5): 296-304.
Rathbone-McCuan, E., and B. Voyles
  1982   "Case Detection of Abused Elderly Parents." *American Journal of Psy-
         chiatry* 139:189-92.
Reece, D., T. Walz, and H. Hageboeck
  1983   "Intergenerational Care Providers of Non-Institutionalized Frail
         Elderly: Characteristics and Consequences." *Journal of Gerontologi-
         cal Social Work* 5(3): 21-34.
Regan, J.J.
  1977   "When Nursing Home Patients Complain: The Ombudsman or the
         Patient Advocate." *Georgetown Law Journal* 65:691-738.
  1981   "Protecting the Elderly: The New Paternalism." *Hastings Law Jour-
         nal* 32:1111-32.
  1983   "Protective Services for the Elderly: Benefit or Threat." Pp. 279-91
         in J.I. Kosberg (ed.), *Abuse and Maltreatment of the Elderly: Causes and
         Interventions.* Boston: John Wright-PSG.
  1985   "Process and Context: Hidden Factors in Health Care Decisions for
         the Elderly." *Law, Medicine and Health Care* 13:151-52.
Ringel Segal, S., and M.A. Iris
  1989   "Strategies for Service Provision: The Use of Legal Interventions in
         a Systems Approach to Casework." Pp. 104-16 in R.F. Filinson and
         S.R. Ingman (eds.), *Elder Abuse: Practice and Policy.* New York:
         Human Sciences Press.
Robertson, G.B.
  1987   *Mental Disability and the Law in Canada.* Toronto: Carswell Company.
Rosenthal, C.J.
  1987   "Aging and Intergenerational Relations in Canada." Pp. 311-42 in
         V. Marshall (ed.), *Aging in Canada: Social Perspectives* (2d ed.). Mark-
         ham, Ont.: Fitzhenry and Whiteside.
Ross, M.M., P.A. Ross, M. Ross-Carson
  1985   "Abuse of the Elderly." *The Canadian Nurse* 81(2): 36-39.
Rounds, L.R.
  1984   *A Study of Select Environmental Variables Associated with Non-Institutional
         Settings Where There is Abuse or Neglect of the Elderly.* Ph.D. disserta-
         tion, University of Texas, Austin.
Rozovsky, L.E.
  1980   *The Canadian Patient's Book of Rights.* Toronto: Doubleday Canada.

Rozovsky, L.E., and F.A. Rozovsky
1987   "Why the Patient's Bill of Rights Is Not a Good Thing." *Health Care* 38.

Sadavoy, J.
1983   "Psychiatric Aspects of Mental Competence and Protection Issues in the Elderly." *Health Law in Canada* 4:1-5.

Salend, E., R.A. Kane, M. Satz, and J. Pynoos
1984   "Elder Abuse Reporting: Limitations of Statutes." *The Gerontologist* 24:61-67.

Sample Survey and Data Bank
1984   *Silence: Description Report of a Follow-up Study of Abused Women Using a Shelter.* Saskatoon, Sask.: University of Regina.

Savage, H., and C. McKague
1987   *Mental Health in Canada.* Toronto: Butterworths.

Schecter, S.
1982   *Women and Male Violence.* Boston: South End Press.

Sengstock, M.C., and S. Barrett
1986   "Elderly Victims of Family Abuse, Neglect, and Maltreatment: Can Legal Assistance Help?" *Journal of Gerontological Social Work* 9(3): 43-61.

Sengstock, M.C., and M. Hwalek
1986   "Domestic Abuse of the Elderly: Which Cases Involve the Police?" *Journal of Interpersonal Violence* 1:335-49.
1987   "A Review and Analysis of Measures for the Identification of Elder Abuse." *Journal of Gerontological Social Work* 10(3/4): 21-36.

Sengstock, M.C., M. Hwalek, and S. Moshiew
1986   "A Comprehensive Index for Assessing Abuse and Neglect of the Elderly." Pp. 41-64 in M.W. Galbraith (ed.), *Elder Abuse: Perspectives on an Emerging Crisis.* Kansas City, Mo.: Mid-America Congress on Aging.

Sengstock, M.C., and J. Liang
1982   *Identifying and Characterizing Elder Abuse.* Unpublished manuscript, Institute of Gerontology, Wayne State University, Detroit, Mich.

Sharpe, G.S.
1983   "Guardianship: Two Models for Reform." *Health Law in Canada* 4:13-23.
1987   *The Law and Medicine in Canada.* Toronto: Butterworths.
1988   "The Protection of Elderly Mentally Incompetent Individuals Who Are Victims of Abuse." Pp. 64-74 in B. Schlesinger and R. Schlesinger (eds.), *Abuse of the Elderly: Issues and Annotated Bibliography.* Toronto: University of Toronto Press.

Shell, D.J.
1982   *Protection of the Elderly: A Study of Elder Abuse.* Unpublished manuscript, Manitoba Council on Aging, Winnipeg, Man.

Sloan, I.J.
1983   *The Law and Legislation of Elderly Abuse.* New York: Oceana Publications.

Social Security Act
    1975   *Social Security Act*, 1975 (Title 20), United States, 1975.
Solomon, K.
    1983   "Victimization by Health Professionals and the Psychologic Response
            of the Elderly." Pp. 150-71 in J.I. Kosberg (ed.), *Abuse and Maltreat-
            ment of the Elderly: Causes and Interventions*. Boston: John Wright-PSG.
Sprey, J., and S.H. Matthews
    1989   "The Perils of Drawing Policy Implications from Research: The Case
            of Elder Mistreatment." Pp. 51-61 in R. Filinson and S.R. Ingman
            (eds.), *Elder Abuse: Practice and Policy*. New York: Human Sciences
            Press.
Stathopoulos, P.A.
    1983   "Consumer Advocacy and Abuse of Elders in Nursing Homes."
            Pp. 335-54 in J.I. Kosberg (ed.), *Abuse and Maltreatment of the Elderly:
            Causes and Interventions*. Boston: John Wright-PSG.
Statistics Canada
    1984   *Current Demographic Analysis: Report on the Demographic Situation in
            Canada in 1983*. (Catalogue No. 91-209E Annual). Prepared by J.
            Dumas. Ottawa, Ont.: Minister of Supply and Services.
    1985   *Population Projections for Canada, Provinces and Territories, 1984-2006*.
            (Catalogue No. 91-520). Ottawa, Ont.: Minister of Supply and
            Services.
Staudt, M.
    1985   "The Social Worker as an Advocate in Adult Protective Services."
            Social Work 30(3): 204-8.
Steel, F.
    1988   "Financial Obligations toward the Elderly: Filial Responsibility
            Laws." Pp. 99-116 in M.E. Hughes and E.D. Pask (eds.), *National
            Themes in Family Law*. Toronto: Carswell Company.
Steinmetz, S.K.
    1978   "Battered Parents." *Society* 15(5): 54-55.
    1983   "Dependency, Stress and Violence between Middle-Aged Caregivers
            and Their Elderly Parents." Pp. 134-49 in J.I. Kosberg (ed.), *Abuse
            and Maltreatment of the Elderly: Causes and Interventions*. Boston: John
            Wright-PSG.
    1988   *Duty Bound: Elder Abuse and Family Care*. Newbury Park, Calif.: Sage
            Publications.
Steuer, J., and E. Austin
    1980   "Family Abuse of the Elderly." *Journal of the American Geriatrics Society*
            28(8): 372-76.
Stevenson, C.
    1985   *Family Abuse of the Elderly in Alberta*. Unpublished manuscript pre-
            pared for the Senior Citizens Bureau, Alberta Social Services and
            Community Health.
Straus, M.A., R.J. Gelles, and S.K. Steinmetz
    1980   *Behind Closed Doors*. New York: Anchor Books.

Townsend, C.
  1971   *Ralph Nader's Study Group Report on Nursing Homes: Old Age — The Last Segregation*. New York: Grossman Publishers.
Townsend, P.
  1981   "The Structural Dependency of the Elderly: Creation of Social Policy in the Twentieth Century." *Ageing and Society* 1:5-28.
Trail, W.R.
  1985   "Elder Abuse: The Costs of Conscience." *Legal Aspects of Medical Practice* 13(6): 5-8.
Turner, T., M.F. Madill, and D. Solberg
  1984   "Patient Advocacy: The Ontario Experience." *International Journal of Law and Psychiatry* 7:329-50.
U.S. Department of Health and Human Services
  1980   *Family Violence: Intervention Strategies*. Human Development Series DHHS Pub. No. (OHDS)80-30258. Washington, D.C.: U.S. Government Printing Office, May.
Valentine, D., and T. Cash
  1986   "A Definitional Discussion of Elder Mistreatment." *Joural of Gerontological Social Work* 9(3): 17-28.
Vladeck, B.C.
  1980   *Unloving Care: The Nursing Home Tragedy*. New York: Basic Books.
Waddams, S.M.
  1984   *The Law of Contracts*. Toronto: Canada Law Book.
Walker, J.C.
  1983   "Protective Services for the Elderly: Connecticut's Experience." Pp. 292-302 in J.I. Kosberg (ed.), *Abuse and Maltreatment of the Elderly: Causes and Interventions*. Boston: John Wright-PSG.
Walker, L.E.
  1984   *The Battered Woman Syndrome*. New York: Springer Publishing Co.
Weller, G.R., and P. Manga
  1982   *Reprivatisation of Hospitals and Medical Care Services: A Comparative Analysis of Canada, Britain and the United States*. Revised version of the paper presented at the 10th World Congress of Sociology, Mexico City, Mexico.
Wellman, B., and A. Hall
  1984   "Social Networks and Social Support: Implications for Later Life." Research Paper #1, Programs in Gerontology, University of Toronto, Research Paper Series, Toronto.
Wilkinson, H.W.
  1986   "Enduring Powers of Attorney Act 1985 and Regulations." *New Law Journal* 136:375-77.
Wills, M., and J.C. Walker
  1981   *Abuse of the Elderly: A Preliminary Report*. Cambridge, Mass.: First National Conference on Abuse of Older Persons, March.
Wolf, R.S.
  1986   "Major Findings from Three Model Projects on Elderly Abuse."

Pp. 219-38 in K.A. Pillemer and R.S. Wolf (eds.), *Elder Abuse: Conflict in the Family.* Dover, Mass.: Auburn House Publishing Co.

Wolf, R.S., M.A. Godkin, and K.A. Pillemer
1984   *Elder Abuse and Neglect: Final Report from Three Model Projects.* Worcester, Mass.: University of Massachusetts Medical Center.

Wolf, R.S., C.P. Strugnell, and M.A. Godkin
1982   *Preliminary Findings from Three Model Projects on Elder Abuse.* Worcester, Mass.: University of Massachusetts Medical Center, Center on Aging.

Yaffe, M.J.
1988   "Implications of Caring for an Aging Parent." *Canadian Medical Association Journal* 138(3): 231-35.

Zborowsky, E.
1985   "Developments in Protective Services: A Challenge for Social Workers." *Journal of Gerontological Social Work* 8:71-83.

Zimberg, S.
1978   "Treatment of the Elderly Alcoholic in the Community and in an Institutional Setting." *Addictive Diseases* 3(3): 417-27.

Zischka, P.A., and I. Jones
1984   "Volunteer Community Representatives as Ombudsmen for the Elderly in Long-Term Care Facilities." *The Gerontologist* 24:9-12.

INDEX

A

Abandonment, 5
Abuse hotlines, 68
Abuse of elderly:
  and depression, 11
  and ethnicity, 19, 90
  and gender, 11, 19, 22, 84, 86
  and health, 86, 89, 100
  and physicians, 53, 56, 64, 69
  and police, 38, 39, 42, 53, 71, 80
  and socio-economic status, 19,
    24, 89
  and tort law, 43, 47
  assistance refused, 92
  by caregiver, 7, 11-12, 19
  by non-caregiver family
    members, 7
  causes of, 23, 35, 89, 101
  "chronic verbal aggression", 6,
    17
  "clean abuse", 43
  counselling for, 71, 92
  definitions of, 2-3, 17, 21, 70, 52,
    83, 88, 90, 97-98, 101
  in nursing homes, 6-7, 17, 20, 23,
    33-34, 42-43, 75, 84, 93
  legal definitions, 8, 18
  material (financial), 3, 4, 17, 34,
    39-40, 46, 89, 101
  measurement of, 5-6, 89, 91
  medical, 5, 38, 89
  passive (neglect), 4, 38, 59, 61,
    80, 85, 89
  physical, 3, 4, 16, 17, 37, 46, 85
  prevalence of, 1, 3, 15, 17, 19
  prevention of, 39-40, 44-45, 46,
    92, 94, 98, 84
  psychological (emotional), 3, 4, 5,
    17, 37, 89
  punishment and, 28

reporting of, by victim, 34, 37, 57
rights of abused, 1, 22, 43, 47,
  51, 57, 61, 63, 64, 69, 72, 97, 99
self-protection against, 43, 49
taxonomy of, 4-5
unintentional, 4, 5, 6
see also Self-abuse, Spouse abuse
Adult day care (respite care), 79,
  100
Adult protection services, 69, 79, 80
Adult Protection Services Program,
  73
"Adult" vs. "elder" abuse, 51-52
Advocacy Centre for Elderly, 38, 73
Advocacy model, 72-75, 76, 81, 99
Aging population, 1, 14
Ageism, 32, 51, 57, 63, 70, 80-81

B

Behavioural model, 2
Benjamin Rose Institute Study, 77

C

Canadian Council on Hospital
  Accreditation, 34
Caregivers, see Abuse, by caregiver
Caregiver dependency, 13, 22, 29,
  84, 86
Characteristics of abused, 10, 11,
  18-19, 84, 90
Characteristics of abusers, 12-14,
  19, 25, 30, 84, 86, 93
Charter of Rights and Freedoms,
  63-64, 65, 98
Child abuse, 1, 21-22, 24, 28
Child welfare model, 49-50, 54, 57,
  60, 64, 69, 70, 79, 97
Chronic care hospitals, 34
Coalition for Nursing Home
  Reform, 42